THE CELL

M000096331

CONTENTS

PREFACE

I am so excited for the opportunity to share my story with so many wonderful people. I believe through the Holy Spirit and God's healing grace; lives will be changed.

This book is my story of God's deliverance of an abandoned un-named baby girl at birth. From age five, I was held hostage by my father and his horrific mental, physical and sexual abuse. He was finally shot and sent to prison. But my unforgiveness and past was my prison.

It's important to realize I had no ability in myself to "forgive" until I became a Christian. Unforgiveness doesn't affect the perpetrator, but the one who is holding on to unforgiveness.

The Bible tells us in 2nd Corinthians 5:17, "Therefore, if any man be in Christ, he is a new creature: old things are passed away, behold, all things become new." Their old life is history. A new life has begun!

My prayer for you is that you will trust God and his Holy Spirit to speak to you today. And I speak "peace" to your heart so that your heart will be open to receiving the love that can only be given by God.

God's love is the beginning of how to give and receive love. God loves each and everyone the same because He is not a respecter of persons.

INTRODUCTION

My wife and I had the blessing of meeting Dana Cryer five years ago in what we describe as a divine appointment. We weren't prepared for the story we heard that night from the sweetest lady in the room. We were instantly drawn to sit next to her because of the Spirit of God living so large in her and continues to connect the three of us today. Our time was brief, but the bond in the Spirit is lasting and has deepened over time.

As Dana told us her story, we were horrified, angered and moved. How could such an atrocity take place to such an innocent child who had no control over her environment or circumstances? As we fought back the rush of emotions, our eyes filled with tears. Dana was peaceful, and her words came across as loving in a way something that can only be described as evidence of God's healing touch and His wholeness that remain obvious to all who meet her. Instead of the bondage and fear that could be expected by the damage from her past. Dana lives a prophetic life today as she carries the healing balm of God's love in each word that presses her heart with God's message. Dana's story is God's Kingdom story expressed in the living Gospel of Jesus Christ; it is as moving as any story told in the Gospel events within the New Testament.

The Good News of God's love indeed does reach into the depths of all our "Emotional Graves" and delivers us from torment and bondage inflicted by the enemy of God in our lives. Dana's story is a stand-up and cheer story that magnifies our champion, Jesus Christ. Dana Cryer has been called to proclaim His good news, declare liberty to the captives; point the way to freedom for those who are oppressed, and announce the year of the Lord's favor.

Today the un-named little girl that was held captive in a cellar has been delivered from her emotional grave and now answers to the name of loving daughter by her daddy God.

Thank you, Dana, for sharing the goodness and love of God's salvation story that has embraced you as his own.

We love you sister,
Rick and Janice Clack

The Cellar, a true-life story of Dana Cryer is a must-read for anyone who has dealt with abuse and neglect. Dana's life-changing testimony is one that was changed from a dark life of abuse to one of celebration all by a loving God! God took her scarred childhood, even young adulthood and transformed it into a living testimony of what the love of God can do for one when there seems no hope left. Dana's compassion to help others is God-given! God took that

THE CELLAR

little broken spirit and changed it into a spirit of compassion and love which is portrayed in every moment of Dana's daily life! As a personal friend of over 20years, her life is a true testimony of what can happen when one turns their life of hurt over to a loving God and let Him do the restoration.

Rev. And Mrs. Rob Bledsoe- Ridgely, Tennessee

Dana's life story is such an amazing testimony of God rescuing someone from one of the worst imaginable situations and turning it all around. The love and goodness of the Father truly brought Dana out of darkness and despair, and into a place of healing and wholeness. Her life is an inspiration to us and many others. We met Dana several years ago, and the words the Holy Spirit spoke to us through her are still impacting our lives and ministry today. She has been a constant source of encouragement to us and many others, but the thing we cherish most is that we get to call this amazing woman of God our friend.

Pastors David and Julie Cantrell SPHR
Abiding Place-Bartlesville, OK

Dana Cryer has been my very best friend for over 45 years. We met as young mothers. Dana was such a loving and kind person. She was on fire for God!! So, soon I was in church praising God with her. We grew in our faith and desired everything God had to offer. Dana is quick to pray and have an encouraging word. God and the scriptures are the foundation of her life. She loves to tell you about her DADDY JESUS and what he has done. The power of forgiveness is life changing!!!

Much love,
Nancy Snider

After having the pleasure of knowing Dana for over 20 years, I know her story is without a doubt the most awe-inspiring, introspective, and supernatural of any I have heard in my 68 years of life. Her story brings us all to exceptional gratitude for our own families and an awe that any human could experience this all in their formative years yet allow God to do such a transformational change to become this amazing woman. As a Naturopathic Physician, I believe she is a walking, ministering miracle because of how I know unforgiveness causes such accumulative maladies in the body. Dana obviously has none because of her tremendous belief and faith in such an awesome God.

Dr. Karen Harris Dial

Dana Cryer

ACKNOWLEDGMENTS

Most of all I thank God for giving me the platform to help His abused children because of His gracious love for them. Whom the Son sets free is free indeed.

I thank my wonderful husband Gene, who has stood with me hand in hand for over forty-five wonderful years. His love and prayers were my strength. Gene, you are truly God's gift to me. Thank you for standing with me during the writing and publishing of this story of my life. As you told me, "If only one person gives their heart to Jesus or gets set free, then it is worth it all." There is no one else I would rather do life with than you. You know my heart. ♡

I am blessed to work with my very special and talented friends. Dean and Sue Brown—they knew my heart and have stood strong with me through this book. They are valued friends.

I thank God for the many friends that have prayed for this book of my life to bless and help the ones that have had the same or similar experiences that I endured as a child.

THE CELLAR

PART ONE

MY STORY

"Although my father and my mother have abandoned me, Yet the Lord will take me up."
Psalms 27:10 AMP

November 5th, 1946

In the middle of the day in a hospital in Flagstaff Arizona I was born in the usual way as any other baby would be. The only unusual thing about my birth was that after bringing me into this world, my mother left me at the hospital. She abandoned me as an infant.

No identity, no bonding with my mother, no comforting cuddles, no adoring grandparents, no aunts, no uncles and no fond memories of a normal childhood.

The one thing I did possess that day, was an incomplete birth certificate. Under "full name of child" were the handwritten words "unnamed baby girl." The name of my father left blank, and the name of my mother was erroneous.

I have no memories **at all** of the time between my birth and the day a man named Earl came into my life when I was five years old.

He approached me while I was on a playground. He must have told me something very inviting because I willingly got into his old beat up station wagon with a small, shiny silver trailer hooked to it.

As it turned out, later I would be left alone in that tiny trailer countless times to fend for myself. But I remember right off, this man from the playground started having sex with me. This man was my father.

Earl lived in an old White House up in the mountains where he had sex with me all the time. Morning, noon, and night. One day followed the next, each one just like the one before it.

He was rough and heavy, forcing me to do things I did not want to do. I had no choice. Never, ever, was I around anyone else. For the next few years, Earl kept me isolated.

During those years of seclusion, I did not attend school. I could not read or write. I did not know that 1 + 1 equals 2. I did not know red and yellow make orange. There were no bedtime stories or favorite children's books.

There were no playmates, no toys, no dolls — no holidays or birthdays. I did not run and play in the sunshine, nor watch TV or listen to music. Earl kept me to himself.

Because I was so young when it all started, my entire being was being shaped by my father. I didn't know anything different. My existence was just sex all the time and focusing solely on taking care of Earl's needs. I had no life, no options, no security, and indeed no love.

What I had was plenty of confusion and fear. And fear is darkness. I distinctly remember the blank darkness surrounding me. It was daily pounded into my head over and over: "Do not tell!"

For about four years, Earl kept me entirely captive for what he desired, whenever he wanted. My young mind could not comprehend, could not answer whether this was right or wrong. But because Earl kept threatening to kill me if I told anyone, this must be wrong.

And also, because he kept telling me that I was a pig, that I was ugly and fat (even though I wasn't), and that I would never amount to anything, his words caused me to begin to consider, "There must be something wrong with me."

Earl's entire existence consisted of his abusing me and his constant drinking. He always smelled of liquor and was continually drunk. Besides that, not only did he use foul language all the time, he was also a compulsive liar. He lied about everything which in turn taught me to do the same.

So it was when I was about seven years old and really should have been in a school like any other child my age, Earl took me driving around during the day looking for things to steal: bicycles, tricycles, or just anything of value. Mostly from oil well sites and farmhouses.

He would scout out other peoples property during the daylight, then go back at night to load up his station wagon with all the items that would fit.

Stealing was how Earl supported himself and his drinking habit. There was never a thought of me having a bicycle or anything close to that. I would not have known how to ride one anyway. And of course, this was a life of continual running. He was always peeling out of parking lots and speeding down the roads for fear of being caught.

Eventually, Earl began to use me to help him steal. He knew just the times to go plundering when no one would be around. Sometimes, because I was smaller and quicker, I would have to climb fences and open gates. Sometime there would be dogs barking.

Then, after carrying off all the loot we could find, the next day Earl would promptly sell the stolen items at a pawn shop. He would immediately take the money, and head to the bars.

Lots of times (when I was with him) during these trips to spy out the goods, it would turn into night, and I would have to sleep in the car while Earl was drinking at a bar. It just didn't matter to him whether the weather was hot or cold. Nor did it matter whether I was hungry or afraid, nor that I was left alone in the back seat of his car.

He just made sure to tell me adamantly that I could not utter one word to anyone about what he was doing to me or regarding his stealing. Earl had to keep me isolated.

However, there was one incident among many in which my father, following his customary night of drinking, was picked up, arrested, and put in jail for DUI. Since I was also in his car, the police put me in a jail cell next to his. Were the police protecting me? Why didn't they care about my welfare? Could they not see how I was being abused?

But then, I wouldn't have told them the truth anyway. I was too afraid to say anything. I had to remain a captive in my own confusing, painful life.

Then one day an unexpected trip took place. Earl brought me to a house where there were other children and a lady named Mary. He again told me that I had better not say anything about what he was doing to me, which I never did out of fear. Fear had become my constant, unwanted companion.

You see, among his other dreadful behaviors, Earl had a horrible temper. And he had a gun. I was terrified of him and had learned not to show any disobedience or emotion towards him.

At Mary's house, I was the oldest among the other children. My stepsister, who was nine months younger than I and three younger boys. Earl Jr., Robert, and James.

Earl and Mary would leave us there alone on occasion. I remember many times standing on a chair with my stepsister to reach the stove in the kitchen, cooking gravy for dinner or whatever I could find.

So not only did I have to meet all of Earl's demands as a nine-year-old child, but I was also put in charge of watching over and feeding these other children.

It became a regular, frightening occurrence that whenever Earl and Mary were together, they would fight. Furniture would sometimes get thrown around and broken.

At these times, I would take the children and try to hide them from all the screaming and fighting. Earl would be violent with Mary, but fortunately not towards the other four children or me.

Things would get so bad between them that I remember hiding with the other children in a dog house in the backyard until things calmed down. It was almost routine; as the police would come and take Earl to jail.

Then Earl and I would leave for a while, but we would always go back to Mary's house. It turns out, Earl was married to Mary and had fathered these other children. Mary was not my biological mother, but my stepmother. And although she was to be my mother figure, Mary never offered me loving care or nurturing assurance. There were no hugs or touches of affection. Not once did I hear "I love you, Dana. Sit on my lap. I saw nothing of "normal" family life.

When we would stay at Mary's place for a while, Earl always made sure I slept closest to the door where he could have me slip out and go somewhere in the house secretly for his sex thing.

Other times I would have to sleep with the window open, and he would tap on the window to signal for me to crawl out. Not surprisingly, I was always afraid to go to sleep wondering if Earl would be coming for me in the night.

When I was ten years old, Earl, Mary, my four half-siblings, and I all moved to a house in Texas. I do not remember whether there were neighbors or how isolated the house may have been.

Regardless, Earl began taking me to the cellar of the home. I do remember how big, abrupt, and heavy he felt while having sex with me and the tremendous fear, dread, and confusion I felt from not being able to control what he was always doing to me.

But one day, a day I remember as shiny and beautiful; I was outside playing with the other children. Clothes were flapping on the clothesline in the gentle breeze. Tumbleweeds were blowing by.

Earl, however, interrupted that beautiful day by showing up and once again taking me to the cellar. Horror filled my being. Would this never end?

But it was on this particular day that Mary decided to go to the cellar herself. She casually opens the cellar door only to discover what Earl was doing to me.

Immediately, Mary ran back into the house screaming at me to stay in the cellar. Falling over himself as well as anything in his path Earl quickly fled up the stairs and out of the cellar. As he was running away, Mary returned and shot him.

The bullet grazed his leg, leaving a bloody trail as he ran off into the canyon behind the house.

In no time, the police were there, and after a small time searching, they apprehended Earl. They also promptly took me to the hospital in another police car.

It was so cold and lonely in that examination room. More fright and confusion followed, as I still remember the doctor who examined me. He then told the nurse that I would probably never be able to have any children of my own. And that I would have some serious mental problems.

With Earl in police custody, I was taken to a temporary place until the state could decide what to do with me. As bad as it was, I had been yanked from the only familiarity I had known and placed into an interim home. A place of real isolation; a holding place for abused kids just like me.

I remember lots of bunk beds in one large room filled with crying kids. I was held there for close to six months. I was not permitted to watch any television due to the massive media coverage taking place at that time concerning my situation.

The shame hidden so long was now coming to light.

While at this home I had to be taught the basics of life, like hygiene and bathing. I'm sure I looked a sight to behold and must have sounded like one, too! I discovered later that court records reported me as poor white trash — another strike against my identity. But I did not know life any other way.

The day finally came when I had to go to court and be a witness against my father. The state found him guilty and sent him to prison.

During the trial, I was terrified to make eye contact with him, but when I did, he angrily mouthed, "I'll get you." Earl was still exerting control and causing the frightening dread I had known so very well from living with him those long, past five years.

Days later the court decided what to do with me and Mary's four children. While we were assembled out front of the courthouse, a boys ranch van picked up Earl and Robert. A Sheriff's car came next for James, who was about five years old and too young to be placed with his brothers in the boys home. I remember that frightened little boy to this day. He was screaming and kicking as they were carrying him off to put in the car. A teddy bear had been placed in the back seat of the car. But James, loudly crying out for me, was not to be consoled by any stuffed animal.

Another car then arrived to pick up my stepsister and myself to take us to a children's home in Amarillo Texas. It was then, at age eleven, I entered the school system by being placed directly in the fifth grade. Remember, I had never been to school before. It was another difficult time in my life.

On top of all this drama, at the same time my stepsister and I were placed in that children's home, my stepmother, Mary, got sick. We were taken to the hospital to see her.

As my stepsister and I entered her hospital room, we found out that she was barely alive and was encased inside an oxygen tent. She looked so bad. She could only write us notes to communicate because at this point she could no longer talk. She was covered with cancer and dying. Oh, the pain we felt.

Now everything had been taken from us — first our three brothers and now Mary. We watched our brothers being taken away by strangers; then we watch Mary being taken away by sickness, for she died while we were in her presence. Her obituary simply stated that she died from a two-week illness.

That night after our painful visit at the hospital, my stepsister and I were driven back to the children's home. The home accommodated three girls to a room, but my stepsister and I were placed together as roommates.

That night after the hospital visit and after the lights had been turned off, I was in my bed crying. So much pent-up emotion had to be released. Everything was confusing. My world as I knew it, had been shaken. The darkness was not a welcome companion, and I felt oh so alone, abandoned once again.

But then the room got bright! I could only think that my house mother had turned on the light. But it wasn't that kind of light. The next thing I saw was an Angel standing at the foot of my bed. The brightness was something I will never forget. Streams of light were as tall as the ceiling, and the Angel was very white. He was beautiful. The Angel then said to me, "Jesus loves you and will always be with you." Thinking my stepsister saw and heard all of this, I couldn't wait to talk about it with her the next morning, but she didn't see or hear anything.

Even though I didn't know Jesus and had not heard of Him, I knew something significant had happened. An Angel visited me. I tucked this special visitation into my heart and would much later have that same message repeated to me at a critical turning point in my life.

I struggled so hard in school. Starting from absolutely no schooling of any kind, then to be placed straight into the fifth grade was torture. Remember I did not even know simple math or the names of things, or the ABCs. How horrible that all the kids could see how dumb I was.

The teacher would always call on me in the classroom, but I never had the answer. I always felt a total blank in my head because I had learned years earlier to show no emotion. I could not even show tears. So my way of coping was to hold everything inside. The most reaction I would show would be clenching my fist. When Earl was having sex with me, I began doing that.

Then at other challenging times, I would clench my fist often to the point of blacking out in my mind.

What was building on the inside would eventually come to the outside and I would black out. My mind would shut down and enter into this blackness. I would become overcome with fear and panic, a feeling so strong that I literally would not be able to hear or see for a while. That would happen anytime I felt unsure or fearful, whether at the children's home or school or practically anywhere.

It was also pointed out to me that when I walked, I clutched my shirt near the neckline with my fist clenched and that even while I was sitting, my fist would become clinched in front of me.

It got to the point that the superintendent over at the school began to notice about how scared I was at school as well as being around other girls and boys my age.

But to me, it was awful knowing that these kids could plainly see the problems I had and how far behind I was. Even the teachers seemed not to have patience with me.

THE CELLAR

Therefore, during my school years, I don't remember ever having any friends. I remember facing more rejection, more feelings of loneliness, and not fitting in. No one liked me; No one wanted me. Something is wrong with me, I thought, having believed that from early on in my life. So much so, that one day in my future this belief would lead me to make a drastic, nearly lethal decision.

Further adding to my pain and fear, certain other men would attempt to make sexual advances towards me whenever I was left alone in their care. Whether at the children's home or on the way to the dentist or to visit an attorney or wherever.

Men continued to exert such control over me, and I began to grow more and more afraid. Great fear, that unwanted companion, came into my life once again. Along with that, I had an overwhelming feeling of dread and horror at having no control over what was being done to me. Will I ever be free from this?

The very worst aspect of this continuing behavior towards me was that after serving his prison sentence, my very own father would be permitted to visit me at the home. And he would try and molest me right there. Unbelievable! He hadn't changed one bit, and he had an uncanny way of locating me.

You see, once a month after church, visitation from friends and family would take place at the children's home where my stepsister and I lived. Every Sunday, all the kids would get onto a bus to attend the local

Presbyterian church that sponsored the home. The boys had to dress nicely, and the girls were required to wear dresses so I would be attired that way.

Certain rooms within the home were set aside for those times of visitation. This way, the child would have privacy with their visitor. Because of this standard procedure, I would be left alone wearing a little dress, behind a closed door in one of those visitation rooms with Earl. The same man with a record of previous crimes against me.

Now and then someone from the home would check on us, but that did not stop my father from trying to touch me inappropriately, nor stop the kissing he forced upon me.

Oh, the torment. Earl was still exerting his awful ways over me. Was there anyone anywhere to protect me?

There were times during my stay at the home when we would be taken to a basement where people from the community donated clothes for the children living there.

This "donated clothes thing" created further embarrassment for me going to school. I was nothing like the other kids. I had no parents, no house to call home, no friends, no regular clothes, and no previous schooling.

Plus I had the painful rejection from potential parents who came to view us for adoption. I can only say that my school years were terrible for me.

But I had one particular teacher who cared. I trusted him enough to talk about some of the things that had happened to me. God bless him!

He would stay after school trying to help me learn something. At the same time, Mother Mae (from the home) was telling me that learning the basics of math and reading would be a skill I would probably never be able to master.

She would take out a ping pong paddle covered with duct tape and paddle me every time she saw my report card.

That one caring teacher, however, new my lack of any previous schooling was why I would almost black out and not know what to say or how to answer questions in the classroom.

He could see the fear that would take over. But this fear also came from a lifetime of abuse and abandonment. Maybe he even knew that, as well.

As an adult, I have thought so many times that as a child my mind could not comprehend what was happening to me.

Earl's years of abuse towards me and that of various other men as well caused me to feel dirty, scared, and fearful of what people thought of me or might do to me.

On top of that, all through my limited years of schooling, I could scarcely read or write. Different people would later ask me, how did you graduate? "Nobody knows," was my reply.

Nevertheless, I was blessed to have graduated from high school in 1965 and got married to a loving man shortly after that.

While still in high school, my stepsister and I attended a local dance. It was there where I met my future husband, Gene. He became my first real boyfriend and the love of my life.

The moment I saw him, I liked him and thought he was cute. It was true love at first sight. He cared about me and loved me immensely and still does to this day. He wanted me to be his wife.

So the time came when I had to leave the children's home after graduation from school at age seventeen. A foster family took me in because I just had nowhere to go and no money to get there. I had no self-esteem and no plans for my future.

But Gene's family, after he told them about me, took me in like I was one of their children and loved me. No questions asked!

This was the first time for me to experience the love of family. Even though Gene's mother already had six children, she loved all of them and me just the same. She was the sweetest, most loving, nurturing woman that ever was. She never complained or had a mean word to say about anyone. I wanted to be just like her when I grew up.

Because we were engaged to be married, it became necessary for me to tell Gene about my abusive past. Not only was it right to tell him and his parents my story, but TV news and local newspapers were filled with the events of my past life anyway. Who in that small town didn't already know this little girl with the abusive father?

I greatly loved and trusted Gene. And I felt safe in his presence. If anything, his knowledge of my abusive father caused him to become even closer to me.

So on May 15th, 1965, Gene and I were married. Here I was, 18 years old and I had never heard the words "I love you." I had never heard words of affirmation from anyone. Because of this, I did not even know how to say "I love you" to Gene. Oh, the things I had to learn.

During the early days of our marriage, Gene did shift work for the oil industry. This meant often being home by myself at night, which was dreadful for me.

Despite the deep love Gene and I had for one another, and how deeply we thought of each other, torment had not departed from my mind. Knowing full well my father was released from prison and very likely to have located me; I was always looking over my shoulder. My mind continually relived scenes from my past life with him, and I was still wondering if my father was nearby.

Too terrified to sleep with my back to the door in my apartment or close to any window, I was also unable to sleep when Gene wasn't home.

What especially kept the impending presence of my father's memory alive was that Gene and I would find out from others in that small Texas town that Earl was fathering more children. Another baby would be birthed with his last name.

And many other things would trigger uncomfortable memories of my past life. Just seeing a small silver Airstream camper being towed would cause my mind to go right back to those frightening days of being left alone in one at the age of five.

My father did intrude into my life at this time. Through his uncanny way of locating me, he let me know he had found me by first making phone calls. I could only slam down the phone not wanting any contact with him. Then he knocked on my door one day, but I wanted nothing to do with him.

He even somehow got our credit card number and dared to spend a tremendous amount of money. We had no recourse but to file a protective order against him.

Gene hated my father. As another form of protection, he wanted to get a dog for me. So, one day we brought home a German Shepherd. We named him Derrick, and from then on, he was always with me. Derrick's presence was comforting and gave me a sense of security. I needed to be able to sleep.

I had always wanted to be a mother, but along with that normal, natural desire, I was severely tormented with thoughts of never being able to bear children. Well, God had another plan. In spite of what had been done to my young body and what doctors may have said, our first son, Brent, was born April 30th, 1968.

Not knowing at the time his future was already planned, someone put a little toy golf set in his baby bed at the hospital when he was born. Someone else brought him a set of yellow Ben Hogan baby clothes that he wore home from the hospital. You see, Brent later went on to become a golf pro.

Then our second son, Brad, was born June 16th, 1972. What a sweet baby, very quiet. Brad just naturally chose to play with toy airplanes when he was quite young. He took flying lessons and became a flight attendant.

Both boys have always respected and loved me. I can genuinely say, I never one time had a desire to harm my little boys in any way. I know that can be a generational curse but thank God that thing was broken. My boys were and are a gift from God.

We moved to Pampa, Texas, when the boys were young. A couple living across the street from our house invited my family and me to church, but only Brent and Brad would go. The boys loved it and soon became born again. My boys would come home and tell me the entire church was praying that I would get born again. But I wanted nothing to do with all that. My heart had a hard shell around it.

I just wasn't in the least interested in any church. I was only interested in pursuing my way of life, which included drinking and parties with people who like to drink.

That hard shell was not softened even after the incident when my boys were five and nine years old, that would have touched almost any mother's heart. It was one particular day when I heard a sound like crying coming from the garage. I rushed in there only to find that my boys were inside a large cardboard box tearfully praying that their mother would get born again. But what did I do? I angrily told them to stop, to come out of there and never do that again.

Plus, in spite of all the kindness shown to me, my heart had no interest in Marilyn either, the neighbor who graciously took my boys to church every Sunday. But I carefully watched her life for two or three years.

As I think back, she was the first Christian influence I had known, yet my stance was to avoid her; I would make every attempt to hide when I saw her coming. I would avoid answering the door when she knocked.

Why was she always so peaceful and kind? And why was she always playing that Gospel music in her car? Why did she have to keep cheerfully inviting me to church with her? Why was she so happy all the time? I only felt conviction around her with my dirty mouth and way of life, yet all the while she was loving me and praying for me.

Marilyn and her husband never preached at me and never judged me. Amidst all the drinking parties at my house, which they would sometimes attend but not drink alcohol, they walked in the pure, unconditional love of God toward me. Marilyn's life shone brightly with the love of God. All the while, I could only think how strange she was, talking about all this Jesus stuff, even though it was she who had so much peace and such a good life.

Marilyn, on the other hand, never lost hope. She was always asking me to go somewhere. Places where people just like her would be, to which I would always say no. But for some reason, one time when asked to go to a tent meeting, I finally agreed and accompanied her.

I had never been to anything like that. A Pentecostal church meeting out in the country in a tent. There were tambourines and dancing, tongue talking and fiery preaching. My eyes must have stayed wide open the entire evening. But this was just a foretaste of what was to take place in my life a few days later.

Before these divine encounters with Marilyn and shortly after moving to Pampa, I took a job at a factory. Down deep inside I was so very unhappy in life. I secretly wanted my life to be over. At the factory, I was always crying from feeling so stupid and at times from not understanding what was happening around me. Plus, I felt like an empty shell of a person, oppressed, dirty, and downtrodden.

All the while though, my boys were in church telling people that their mom needed to be born again. People were there at that church who cared about me and prayed for me without ever meeting me. Those prayers were soon to be actualized.

Work at the factory was just as you might imagine. Every day I stood in an assembly line, my coworkers and I just an arm's length apart. However, we could not talk to each other; we could only focus on the routine of accurately filling our quota.

But even if we could talk to one another, it was so loud in there that it was impossible to hear what was being said. As loud as the machinery was and as repetitive as the manual labor was, a sound louder and more repetitive was the one in my head.

Remember, I felt unlearned, unclean and unimportant. A pattern of wrong thinking had grown in me since childhood, and it only became worse during this time. Anger and hatred coupled with fear and self-doubt, along with self-loathing and unforgiveness were a recipe for self-destruction waiting to happen.

So, it was inevitable that a continual barrage of tormenting thoughts plagued my mind day after day with voices that told me to kill myself. Those voices grew louder and louder telling me, "Walk in front of a truck. Why not go jump in the nearby Lake?" The voices were so loud that I could feel a presence on my shoulder talking in my ear all the time saying, "Kill yourself."

One particular day while at the factory the torment was so overpowering that I just had to leave my place at the assembly line and go into the restroom. I looked in the mirror to see a distorted, wild look on my face and in my eyes. I looked terrorized. Instantly I started screaming, "Stop! What is this? What is happening to me?" What was happening was lying spirits were tormenting me with their fear.

After so many episodes like this, the time came that I believed those relentless thoughts. Suicide began to seem like the only solution.

Terminating my life would be the only way to put an end to my shame and confusion once and for all. Fear and torment would end also.

So, one evening at home when Gene took the boys to football practice, I decided to pursue the plans in my life. As I did, it was as if every detail to carry out this deed was given to me in a script to follow, such as in a movie, even to the point of putting a red spread on the bed.

Plus, I had made it a point to clean the house thoroughly that weekend because I knew people would eventually be coming in there to find me dead. I even thought that the red spread on the bed where I would die wouldn't be so hard to clean since it was as red as my spilled blood would be.

Now, I needed to get a gun, and I knew where one was. I would end my life with a gunshot. Just a few footsteps away was a gun.

However, just as I was starting down the hall to get the gun, my mind intent on killing myself, the phone rang. It was Marilyn, of all people. Marilyn, the neighbor from across the street who had been taking my sons to church and from whom I used to hide, called to tell me that Jesus loved me and would never leave me.

That was all she said, making this the second time I had heard this message from God. Upon hearing this from Marilyn, I instantly thought of the angelic visitation I had had while in the children's home, as the exact words were spoken to me then.

We hung up the phone, and as I went back into my bedroom, the room suddenly lit up with the same kind of light from an Angel as I had seen as a child! I tell you, I had some severe problems. But when I went into my bedroom, I had such a visitation. Bright lights streamed down to fill my room, and I heard a heavenly choir. It felt like a hand gently pushing me down on to my bed. So, there on the red bedspread laid out for an entirely different purpose, I cried hard with deep weeping for a long time.

God was there, and I wanted Him. O how I now wanted Him. I was indeed at the end of myself and could now receive God. His glory and all that God is was in that room. The room seemed saturated with so much of God's love, and I quickly ask Him to come into my heart.

And thanks to all the times my sons would rush home from church excitedly telling me about God's gift of Salvation, I knew what to do. "If you confess with your mouth that Jesus is Lord and believe in your heart that God raised

Him from the dead, you will be saved. For it is by believing in your heart that you're made right with God, and it is by confessing with your mouth that you are saved." (Romans 10:9-10 LT).

There was never a time in my life that I cried like that. So deeply and for so long that it turned into groaning. I was feeling such deep-seated pain. My pain spanned a lifetime. I had never experienced anything like this depth of release.

The love I felt pouring into my heart was so beautiful. I had so much anger, so much hatred and negative emotion inside that I was not able to cry to that degree. My heart had turned to stone and could not release anything buried so deeply. Remember, my father had prevented me from ever showing emotion. October 2nd, 1978, I wept. Hurtful things were being pulled out of me, while God's love poured into me.

While this was happening in my heart, Marilyn was prompted to come to my house. When she arrived, she explained that shortly after phoning me, God had told her to go to my house and pray with me. She got to share the awesome experience of life in transformation.

But before she arrived, the Godly presence in my bedroom felt like someone was getting ready to touch me. And at that moment, even though I did not know one thing about Jesus or the Holy Spirit, my hands went up, and while crying, some sounds came out of my mouth I could not identify.

"And they were all filled with the Holy Ghost and began to speak with other tongues, as the Spirit gave them utterance." (Acts 2:4 KJV).

I had been born again. "For God so love the world so much that He gave His one and only Son so that everyone who believes in Him with will not perish but have eternal life." (John 3:16 NLT).

I had become spiritually changed. "Anyone who belongs to Christ has become a new person. The old life is gone; a new life has begun." (2nd Corinthians 5:17 NLT).

His saving power, awesome love, and mercy through Jesus Christ transformed such a hideous life into a life like I now have.

His Salvation provided such cleansing from feeling dirty; such overflowing peace from tormenting fear; such abundance of joy from humiliating shame; such soundness of mind from relentless unrest; and such limitless love from bitter hatred. My stony heart had become softened.

When Marilyn arrived at my house, she began to cry with joy over me. We prayed together; we celebrated together the most significant miracle anyone can experience in life: The gift of Salvation. But God is so rich in mercy, and He loved us so much that even though we were dead because of our sins, He gave us life when He raised Christ from the dead. "For it is only by God's grace that you have been saved." (Ephesians 2:4-5 NLT).

And scripture also says, "God saved you by His grace when you believed, and you can't take credit for this; it is a gift from God. Salvation is not a reward for the good things we have done, so none of us can boast about it." (Ephesians 2:8,9 NLT).

The next morning, I had to find the Bible Gene had bought for me many years earlier. I was now seeking life, not death! And with all this, a new interest in love for the Word of God was compelling me.

"Thy words were found, and I did eat them; and thy Word was unto me the joy and rejoicing of my heart." (Jeremiah 15:16 KJV). Neither could I wait to get into a church.

As soon as the next service time began, Marilyn took me to church with her family and my boys. I walked into the church only to find everyone was celebrating. They were celebrating what had just happened to me. Not only that, they had water baptism ready for me. It was there that I met a wonderful, loving pastor and his wife, Susie, who upon meeting me took me in with open arms and acceptance. Susie befriended me right away and began to call me often to pray with me and to ask if I had questions.

After a lifetime of despair and mental suffering, fear, and shame, within one week I experience the awesomeness of God first at a tent meeting, then in my bedroom, and now at a loving church. It was only the beginning of an inspiring, fulfilling, and purposeful life with

God. He had many things yet to show me and do with me.

This new life with God through Jesus, His Son, continued with God giving me dreams. The very first dream was merely amazing and revealed to me how real God is in every person's life no matter the circumstances, no matter the evil or the prosperity. I dream that I was walking toward a big white house.

I dreamed that I was walking toward a big white house. On the front porch, I saw a man rocking a baby and rubbing the baby's back. I could hear Him telling the baby how much he loved the baby.

As I walked closer, I knew it was Jesus. The baby then turned and looked at me.   That baby

"I knew you before I formed you in your mother's womb" Jeremiah :1:5

was ME!

THE CELLAR

Wow! God moved so fast to help me understand who he was in my new life. I could not wait to call Susie, my pastor's wife.

Maybe two nights later I had another dream. I was at home, and lots of people were coming to my house. I noticed everyone was rolling up their pant legs before they entered.

When they came in, water rose up to their knees. There was much joy and laughter among the people in my house.

Jesus spoke to me, "If you only knew the gift God has for you and who you are speaking to, you would ask Me, and I would give you living water." (John 4:10 NLT).

I called Susie again and told her about the dream. She said it was the Holy Spirit with springs of living water. Cleansing and healing. "But those who drink the water I give will never be thirsty again. It becomes a fresh, bubbling spring within them, offering eternal life." (John 4:14 NLT).

Exciting things were happening to me. To me! Just a week of new life in Christ, I knew it was a good thing, and it was indeed real. "The teaching of your Word gives light, so even the simple can understand." (Psalms 119:30 NLT).

And God was always waking me during the night to tell me something. One of the first things he spoke to me was, "Eyes and ears. Eyes and ears." I thought. What? Eyes and ears?

I got out of bed, went into the living room turned on the light, opened the Bible and it just fell open to what scripture means when it says, "No eye has seen, no ear has heard, and no mind has imagined what God has prepared for those who love Him." (1st Corinthians 2:9 NLT).

It was in this manner that God began to teach me. He would wake me at night and tell me many things. Not only that, but it was also God who increased my reading skills with the Bible.

So, then it was, the King James Bible my husband had bought me years earlier became my ever-constant companion. I started reading it nonstop! I had an insatiable hunger for the Word of God. Don't tell me God can't give us an understanding of His Word. I would cry so much because I understood this was a love letter to me. I needed to read so I could learn who I was as a Christian.

Funny thing though, because I thought all Christians had this same thing going on in their lives. I was so happy and excited and just wanted to run and tell everyone what I was seeing, reading, and dreaming. But I quickly became surprised that not everyone wanted to hear.

So, I told Susie and my pastor all that was going on. They were happy for me and would have discussions with me explaining further what this new life in Christ was all about.

Not much later I met a lady named Nancy, and our first meeting was not particularly friendly. Not only had she and her family just started going to the same church I was attending, but she also lived right across the street from me in the same house where Marilyn had recently moved out. (Marilyn was the one who had been instrumental in leading me to Jesus.) It was no accident, and I was determined to meet Nancy.

Even though one of her daughters told me that her mother thought I was weird, I pressed harder to get to know her.

Much like Marilyn had been with me, I too, witnessed to Nancy all the time. I continually told her how great God was as well as all the incredible things he was doing in my life.

My excitement simply could not be contained. And like I had previously acted around Marilyn, Nancy tried to avoid me. I would not stop talking about God. I had become a Marilyn in Nancy's life.

But before too long, Nancy and I'd did become friends. And so, it was, one day she and her husband were returning from a shopping trip at the local mall when Nancy told her husband, "I have to go to Dana's house." She called first and said she was supposed to come by.

As Nancy came into my house, she quickly explained that she did not know why she was there but that I had to pray for her. She also revealed she just wanted to know if God was real and if all the great things I had been telling her for the past several days were real. I laid hands on Nancy and prayed with her, then told her to go home and read Jeremiah 33:3 which says, "Ask Me, and I will tell you remarkable secrets you do not know about things to come."

When Nancy returned home, she read that passage but was led to read John 14:14, "If ye shall ask anything in my name, I will do it." Alright, she thought and spontaneously lifted her hands and started speaking in tongues. Such was the flow she could not stop the tongues which poured out for hours! Nancy has never lost that enthusiasm.

What's so important about this experience with Nancy is that I had just read Acts chapter two in the Bible about the laying on of hands. Believe and receive — what a miracle. The thing is, I genuinely believe what I read in the Bible was for me. It was a childlike faith. Nancy thought this way too. She and I would read the Bible, then get on our faces and pray for hours wanting what we read.

What a dear and faithful friend! I talked to Nancy often, even though we now live in different states, and we have been close friends for more than 30 years.

Nancy and I just grew and grew in the Lord during this time at each other's house and at that little church in Texas where we met. Several times a year this church would host special speakers.

One night, a particular guest speaker was praying and laying hands on people. He called me to the front to speak over me. Well, I wanted and was expecting for Him to impart the gift of healing (that is laying hands on the sick) and the gift of prophecy, which I thought were the great gifts.

As he laid his hands on me, he stopped and suddenly told me that I had the gift of love. I said, "What?" He then said, "I've never seen this before, the spirit of love."

God proceeded to touch my heart, and that night He filled me head to toe with His love. I did not know what a great gift this was. Indeed, this was the greatest gift of all. It was years later that I understood how powerful God's kind of love is.

With all the great things happening in my life, after a while, darkness came. Sometimes when I would take afternoon naps or be asleep at night when Gene, my husband, was not at home, something heavy like rubber would lay on me. Because this "thing" would hold my mouth closed, I couldn't scream. I couldn't do anything when this would happen to me for it exerted such pressure on my chest and my body as to hold me motionless. Now, this thing was not visible nor discernible, except that it was evil.

When this would occur, which was oddly almost always during the day and was increasing in frequency, I kept asking God in my mind to help me.

Again, I could not utter a sound with the weight of this thing on me, so in my mind, I would ask "God, what do I do? I pray; I resist, but this thing is still tormenting me". God would reply, "Say, the blood." I would repeat, "The blood of Jesus" in my thoughts and the thing would leave. Afterward, however, I would be completely drained of energy.

Even though this thing visited me many times, I never told anyone, feeling too embarrassed to say to them that during these horrible times, a heaviness was holding me down and it felt like sexual abuse.

It was during this same time when I was so used of God, traveling and speaking in churches, that I could not admit I was going through this awful occurrence. Not me, born again and so free. Pride would not let me tell of it. But one day after church, some ladies and I were talking.

Somehow during the conversation, I brought up this mysterious matter, and one of the ladies said she had experienced the same thing!

I continued to pray that God would show me what this thing was. Then one day on television, it just so happened the word "incubus" appeared on the screen. Because of the nature of the TV program, I was prompted to look in the dictionary at this strange word.

It turns out, this tormenting spirit that visited me many times is called an incubus spirit! Webster's dictionary defines it as an evil spirit that lies upon people in their sleep; one that has sexual intercourse with women while they're sleeping; one that oppresses or burdens like a nightmare.

A nightmare indeed! Webster's dictionary also defines "nightmare" as "an evil spirit formally thought to oppress people during sleep; a frightening dream accompanied by a sense of oppression or suffocating that awakens the sleeper; a feeling of anxiety or terror."

Wow! When I read that definition, I knew how Satan was trying to bring the past to me again. But you know why? I had not honestly let go of the past either. What I mean is, I had yet to forgive my father.

But one day as this invasive presence continued to visit me; Nancy called knowing something was wrong. I finally told her about this invading spirit, and she came right over, anointed me with oil, and rebuked the incubus spirit. Nancy and I were still so new to faith in God, but we got our Bibles and started reading.

The Bible told us God was our Helper in time of need, so we turned to Him in this time of great need. The Bible also told us, "Behold, I give unto you power to tread on serpents and scorpions, and over all the power of the enemy: and nothing shall by any means hurt you." (Luke 10:19 KJV). "And ye shall know the truth, and the truth shall make you free." (John 8:32 KJV).

We knew to speak the Word of God out loud until we got free from this spirit.

We prayed, "Father, your ears are open to our cry. You said if any two agree, we shall ask, in the Name of Jesus, and it shall be done." As the Bible says, "Again I say unto you, that if any two of you shall agree on earth as touching anything that they shall ask, it shall be done for them of my father which is in heaven. For where two or three are gathered together in my name, there am I in the midst of them." (Matthew 18:19-20 KJV).

We continued to pray, "We believe, Lord Jesus, that according to your Word the devil has come to steal, kill, and destroy. "But God has come to give us life more abundantly." (John 10:10) "and that you will never leave us nor forsake us." (Hebrews 13:5)."

After that time of prayer, that evil presence visited one more time, and I had had enough.

Nancy came, put my Bible on my chest. I made a line with my foot and told the devil to come on. I had the Word of God in my mouth, the anointing of the Holy Spirit, and bless God; I won that battle once and for all. That evil spirit never returned.

Now all through the years of being born again and during my times of reading the Bible, God would show me scriptures concerning forgiveness. Plus, I would even purposely look up and spend time reading Bible verses about forgiveness. I knew it was a Bible command for Christians to forgive those who have wronged us, and I deeply grieved over my father's misconduct.

While doing this, conviction to forgive him would come, but I could not pardon my father's abusive, ruinous behavior towards me.

Howbeit, holding onto unforgiveness was a severe weight to carry because it turned into bitterness and resentment. Yes, Earl had broken the law and served time; but wasn't I breaking God's law?

After much study of the Bible and struggle within myself, the day finally came when I said in my heart, I forgive my father. Not long after my decision to forgive, I was asleep on the sofa and awake and for some odd reason. A vision promptly came in which I saw God holding my father in one of his arms, and me in the other.

I then saw God look at Earl and heard Him say, "I forgive him." Next, God looked at me and said, "Now you forgive him."

I fell on my face, and oh, such crying and travailing deep within me occurred as all the years of anger, pain, and hatred was released. To be replaced with incredible love and forgiveness for my father. Tears of forgiveness cleansed me from all the things that were residing deep in my heart and love that I had never had for my father filled me. "Since God chose you to be the holy people He loves, you must clothe yourself with tenderhearted mercy, kindness, humility, gentleness, and patience." (Colossians 3:12 NLT).

Because my half-stepsister occasionally stayed in touch with me over the years, it was through her I knew where my father lived and had his phone number. After God showed me that vision of forgiveness, the time soon came when I called Earl and told him I forgave him.

He listened respectfully as I also explained that I was born again and told him all about my beautiful, new life with God and that I desired he had this new kind of life also. I explained salvation to him and then mailed him a Bible and salvation literature along with a letter I had written.

Meanwhile, on a Wednesday night at church with my family, I was tapped on the shoulder, and the usher whispered to me and told me I had a phone call. My stepsister had called to inform me that Earl had died from a heart attack.

My husband and I drove to Houston, Texas, for the funeral, but along the way, I prayed that God would somehow show me that Earl had received Christ before he died.

When we arrived at his house, I went into his bedroom and on the headboard of his bed was the Salvation literature I had sent and an open Bible. Praise the Lord!

I genuinely believe anyone, no matter who or under what circumstance, can get born again by asking Christ into their heart. God made the way to Himself simple. If you confess with your mouth that Jesus is Lord and believe in your heart that God raised Him from the dead, you will be saved.

"For it is by believing in your heart that you are made right with God, and it is by confessing with your mouth that you are saved, for everyone who calls on the name of the Lord shall be saved." (Romans 10:9-10, 13 NLT).

The Bible teaches much about salvation and forgiveness, faith and love, but also about the consequences of sin.

I know that all the anger, hate, and unforgiveness I had in my heart was not any different from the incest my father committed. Without Jesus, we would all be lost and separated from God eternally.

People would always angrily ask me how I could forgive such an offender as my father. How could I excuse such abuse and misuse? That man wrecked my life, how could I pardon him?

My reply would always be, Jesus Christ forgave me. I have to do the same. I never argue nor debate. I explain it is only by the transforming power of the Word of God and prayer and that even though it took time and I fought for it, forgiveness is one of the most liberating things a Christian can and must do.

"But I say unto you, love your enemies bless them that curse you, do good to them that hate you, and pray for them which despitefully use you, and persecute you." (Matthew 5:44 KJV).

The Bible tells us to walk in love towards the people who abuse us, abandon us, or hurt us. That is obeying God's Word and walking in Jesus' love the way He loves us.

The most amazing part of this was that my father asked Jesus into his heart a short time after I called to tell him that I forgave him. That occurred right before he died of a massive heart attack at the age of 58. And I can honestly say I know I will see him in heaven.

The miraculous events were to continue. The year was 1984. One particular Mother's Day while I was in church, the pastor asked all the mothers and their daughters to come to the front for celebration and prayer. I was watching them assemble at the front.

I immediately became distraught and felt intense pain from not being able to know the joy these women had, despite the knowledge that my mother did not want me, had abandoned me and was absent my entire life.

At age thirty-seven, I still had a strong desire to meet her. Where was she? What was she like? I wished she were near. That Mother's Day the desire consumed me, and I prayed, "God, what about my mother? I would love to know who my mother is."

It turns out later at home; I located a piece of crumpled, torn paper I had received when Earl died. It had my birth information on it. It said "unnamed baby girl" and stated my mother's name as Mary Ann Cervantes, Coco Neil County, Flagstaff.

I also recall during my years at the children's home after Earl's arrest, that now and then I would somehow hear the name

Cervantes spoken. It did not make sense to me then.

Perhaps during the time of his arrest and trial, Earl had told the police the actual name of my mother. I also remember Earl telling me early on that my mother was a no-good person and not to think about her. Nevertheless, like a jigsaw puzzle, the pieces of my past life were about to fit together.

I quickly dialed the telephone operator and asked for the number of Mary Ann Cervantes. The operator replied, "Ma'am, there are lots of people with the last name Cervantes, but I will give you one of the numbers, and maybe they'll know her." I jotted down the number and hung up.

Well, that night after church, I returned home and dialed that number. It was still Mother's Day. A young girl answered the phone, and I asked, "Does a Mary Cervantes live there?" The little girl called out, "Grandma, someone wants to talk to you."

A voice then said, "Hello." I cheerfully replied, "Happy Mother's Day." "Who are you," she inquired? I responded, "Did you have a daughter thirty-seven years ago?" and told her my father's name.

She instantly burst into tears, and so did I. And for all the joyful crying, we could no longer talk! Mary was my mother, whom I had never seen but had always yearned to meet someday. Talk about an answer to prayer! And from just that very morning at church. I could not believe the joy I felt.

My mother and I proceeded to get acquainted through several phone conversations over a short period. To this day though, I do not know how news of reuniting with my mother traveled so fast.

Just days after meeting my mother by phone, I was at my desk at work when a paid-in-full round-trip airplane ticket to Flagstaff, Arizona, was delivered to me. At long last, it was time. I was going to meet my mother.

Overjoyed I also wanted a traveling companion to make this very important trip with me. My husband could not get away from his work and Brent, my older son, was committed to playing in a football game.

Therefore, my younger son, Brad, who was then about twelve years old, accompanied me, also with a paid-in-full airline ticket provided anonymously.

As we landed in Arizona, I was becoming more nervous and excited that this meeting was happening. I could hardly sit still and had a flock of butterflies in my stomach.

Upon arriving at the Flagstaff airport, I called a taxi to take my son and me to my mother's house. The taxi driver was most friendly and helpful, and in merely making conversation, he said: "What brings you to Arizona"? I answered, "This is just nothing short of a miracle," and briefly told him how I found my mother on Mother's Day and that we were about to meet for the first time since I was born.

After I finished telling him my story, the driver became very emotional as he asked if his wife who works for the local newspaper could meet us, write a story and take some pictures to be published in the paper. I politely declined because of potentially putting my mother in an awkward position of not yet having met me.

Besides, this moment was so important as well as sacred. I thought it should be kept private until we knew each other better. However, it was not long after our initial meeting that an article and a photograph was published in a local magazine in the town where I lived in Texas.

Another reason I declined the publicity was that previously during our second phone conversation, my mother informed me I had half-brothers and a stepsister, but she had never once mentioned to them I had been born.

She now had to tell them about me! My stepbrother, whom I eventually met, was excited to meet me; my stepsister was not ready to. I felt it was just better; the public did not yet know about this miraculous family reunion.

The special moment, anticipated for a lifetime, finally arrived. As the taxi pulled up to my mother's house, the driver explained, "We're here."

Before we arrived at Mom's house, I had mentioned to the driver that the company I work for in Pampa Texas had given me a camera for my special trip and would he take a picture for me to keep for myself. "Of course," he said.

My mother was waiting on her front porch with a close friend of hers and the friend's daughter. As soon as my mother saw me get out of the taxi along with my son, she left the porch and came towards us.

We instantly embraced each other long and hard, and in doing so, I smelled her cologne. It was the very same cologne I had worn for years. Imagine that! I told her that was my Cologne of choice and she said that was the only one she ever wore. Not only did we have that in common, but many other similarities were discovered as the night wore on.

Later that evening, my mother and I, as well as the friend and daughter were sitting around the kitchen table after enjoying dinner together. Mother's friend showed love to me as much as if I were her missing daughter coming home. The conversation eventually led to my mother wanting to know all about me.

I told her everything from Earl taking me away at the age of five, to the abusive behavior and extreme isolation, to the chain of events that led to his arrest, to my difficult years at the children's home and school, up to my marriage to a wonderful man and our two sons.

During my recounting my life story, everyone at the kitchen table was crying. That is everyone except Brad who was in another part of the house watching television.

However, I found it a little odd that the teenage daughter was upset and crying at hearing my story. It was not until later that evening I found out why.

But before that time, yet another oddity became evident throughout our conversation; I grew more and more amazed how very much like my absentee mother I was. Besides the same cologne we preferred, we chose similar clothing styles of bright colors. Plus, we both belong to the same kind of Pentecostal church.

We both love to be hospitable by always preparing large amounts of food, ever ready to serve the numerous people who would randomly drop by.

And of greater importance, we both individually became born-again close to the same time and upon similar kinds of circumstance. My mother had suffered from so much guilt and shame for abandoning me and for the path in life which she took, that she too had suicidal intentions that were intervened by the loving God of the Bible. She chose to live, not die, by calling out to Him and got born again as I did.

Mothers friends soon left, for we were all worn out from the day's hearts-stirring conversation. I finally got into bed only to be awakened by my mother a short time later. It was 1:30 AM.

Strangely, she could not say my name the entire time I was at her home. She just called me "Hon." "Hon, wake up." I need you to come into the den. Sleepily, I crawled out of bed and followed my mother not knowing what to expect.

The same lady and her teenage daughter who was present earlier that day and throughout that evening were sitting in the den. They looked quite distressed, and both were virtually wailing. I quickly thought back at how the daughter had cried when I was telling my life story previously at the kitchen table.

It turns out that the young girl had only just informed her mother for the first time on their way home that evening, that her father was doing the same to her. Her father was molesting her sexually, and no one knew it.

She was able to tell her story to me as it came pouring out of her like a swiftly moving river and when she finished, the first thing I did was ask if she wanted to know Jesus.

Yes, she answered promptly, and we prayed for her salvation and then we prayed again, this time for wisdom for her and her mother.

After a few priceless days in my mother's house, the time came when I had to return home. But by telling my story on that first day, I allowed other people into a dark secret, which then paved the way for another victim of the same kind of abuse to find a way out—a way out of the shame, guilt, and despair through

Jesus Christ. This proves we never know when God has someone that needs our testimony.

I have since had so many women tell me that they came from a Christian home with great parents and they felt like they had no testimony. Wow! How blessed they are to be able to say that. But, they need to know they still have a walk with God that's worth telling a hurting world. They do have a testimony of how faithful God is day by day throughout their lifetime no matter what.

I was most fortunate to have visited my mother in Flagstaff when I did and to see her one more time because, within a year of initially meeting her, she died from health problems. Yes, I was saddened, and it was a loss, but like my father's passing, I took comfort knowing I would see my mother again in heaven.

As I tell this story today, I feel so blessed because we do not know how our lives are going to be a blessing to someone later. I know that I have a sacred walk with Jesus. It is hard to put into words, but to know Jesus the way I do is so wonderful.

To have been broken, abused, and fearful, and yet God put this particular scripture in the Bible for me, "Even if my father and mother abandon me, the Lord will hold me close." (Psalms 27:10 NLT).

When my father and mother forsake me, then the Lord will take me up. He will gather me up. Wow! That is why I started calling Jesus my Daddy. "He will feed his flock like a Shepherd.

He will carry the lambs in His arms, holding them close to His heart." (Isaiah 40:11).

Relax in His everlasting arms. The eternal God is your refuge, and underneath is His everlasting arms. God is so aware of you that when you are weak, He is strong. Let Him carry you when you have no energy.

God would say to you today, "Rest in Me. Refresh yourself in my presence." Let go of cares and worries so that you can receive His peace. Open your heart and mind to receive all He has for you.

God wants you to talk to Him about your struggles, your fears, your family, or your sickness. Just be honest and tell Him you are in pain, not understanding what to do. He loves when you empty yourself and let Him in to fill you with His peace, His comfort, and the knowledge that all is well.

PART TWO

LIVING IN HIS LIGHT

"I am the light of the world. He that followeth me shall not walk in darkness but shall have the light of life." (John 8:12).

MY LIFE TODAY

I have had the honor of speaking and teaching in church services, including prayer meetings and women's meetings, in numerous churches throughout Texas, Oklahoma, Missouri, and Louisiana. During these times I've witnessed many salvations and healings in people of all ages. God has used my life story to testify of his amazing grace and unconditional love.

Since being born again, I have always ministered to anyone about Jesus and have loved sharing my story of having been abandoned and forsaken but not forgotten by God. Everyone needs to know that God loves them right now and that He has wonderful things to give them. He has Salvation and healing and deliverance and peace to give.

Don't be afraid! Speak out! Don't be silent! "For I am with you, and no one will attack and harm you, for many people here in this city belong to me." (Acts 18:9-10 NLT).

Also, as miraculous was being taught to read by God with the Bible, so was being trained by Him to become a massage therapist as a ministry unto Him. Many people came to me for several years for relaxation or pain relief in their bodies. Ministers and church leaders, as well as people from all walks of life, came for my services. I was able to tell my story to numerous clients and listen to theirs which paved the way for personal ministry and prayer.

Another significant experience in my life was that of being interviewed on the 700 Club with Pat Robertson. God had previously told me that I would tell my story on television one day and that my book would be written. It was indeed God that opened the way for my TV appearance, and now a book has been written. Watching this happen shows that God directs our steps for higher purposes. If he says it, he will do it.

After retiring from massage therapy, I learned to play golf with my husband. My older son, Brent, as you may remember from my story, is a pro golfer and my younger son, Brad, enjoys playing also. I love the sport and being with my guys, but the places it takes me, and the people I meet are excellent opportunities to speak about God.

THE CELLAR

Always, always someone needs to hear about Jesus. God knows just who to place in our path for us to talk about Him. Be ready and watchful for those open doors to tell of God's goodness and love.

God is continually showing me how faithful He is. I have seen His promises coming alive daily since I ask Him into my heart.

If I've learned anything these past several years, it is this; not to worry about one thing. Not to worry about myself, my family, anything. I am free from trying and from wasting time worrying. God is trustworthy, and He is able.

God teaches us such simple ways and things. One time, my husband took one of our grandsons, Nick, fishing. Nicholas was three years old at the time and had a hard time releasing the fishing line. My husband kept saying, "Release it, Nick." He was struggling with what he had heard his Papa say, not knowing what he was releasing. He stood nearby watching Papa and all at once Nick said, "Oh Papa, I get it now. I need to let the line go." At three years old, he understood it. God, please teach us the way you did with Nick, to let go of anything we do not understand.

That is what God wants us to do. Watch Him until we learn to let it go. Let go of all the things that worry us, and that seems troublesome or difficult to understand. When we let go, God can then take care of it.

I thank God for my wonderful husband, Gene, and that we have been married for more than fifty-four years. We raised two fine boys who have their own beautiful families and who are all born again. Even though I had many problems during our early years of marriage, Gene had the grace to stay with me. He also had God's favor to be able to understand me when I didn't. God bless my husband, for when I was not lovable, he loved me.

I also want to mention that I had the ultimate privilege of leading my three grandsons to the Lord when they were around five and six years old by telling them how much Jesus loved them. I cannot think of anything else that could make me happier. Nick, Cade, and Jace all walk in so much love and are full of the Lord. What an eternal joy to my heart. God will show Himself to you today. Believe and receive. I pray this for you. God bless you.

"I was born a sinner. Yes, from the moment my mother conceived me." (Psalms 51:5). We all have to be born again!

I pray as you read my story; you will see your need for a Savior. That Savior is Jesus Christ. All anyone has to do is confess with your mouth that Jesus is Lord and believe in your heart that God raised Him from the dead; you will be saved. "For anyone who calls on the Name of the Lord will be saved." (Romans 10:9,13).

Jesus tells us He stands at the door of our heart and knocks. "Here I stand at the door and knock. If you would hear Me calling and open the door, I will come in, and we will share a meal as friends." (Revelation 3:20).

We are instantly in the family of God when we ask Him into our hearts. Jesus also tells us, "I will give them eternal life, and they will never perish. No one will snatch them away from Me, for my Father has given them to Me, and He is more powerful than anyone else. So, no one can take them from Me." (John 10:28-29).

The most important thing you do after praying and asking Jesus in your heart is to get a Bible, and the Holy Spirit will teach you all about his wisdom and knowledge. We need to grow in Him. Reverent fear of the Lord is the foundation of real understanding. All who obey His commandments will grow in wisdom. Reverence for the Lord is the foundation of true knowledge. The rewards of knowledge come to all who follow Him. Praise His Name forever (Psalms 111:10).

The Kingdom of God is entered only by the new birth. What this means is that those who become Christians become new persons.

"They are not the same anymore for the old life is gone. A new life has begun." (2nd Corinthians 5:17). Wow, that is straight from God's mouth to us because we accepted Him as our Lord Jesus Christ.

"All this newness of life is from God, who brought us back to Himself through what Christ did. And God has given us the task of reconciling people to Him. For God was in Christ, reconciling the world to Himself, no longer counting peoples sins against them. This is the beautiful message that He has given to us to tell others." (2nd Corinthians 5:18-19).

I did not even know that I was doing this when I was born again, but I wanted to tell everyone about this great feeling I had. I knew after I had come out of my bedroom in 1978 that I was different, and when you become born again, you will also find your heart feels so much better.

"For it was I, the Lord your God, who rescued you from the land of Egypt. Open your mouth wide, and I will fill it with good things." (Psalms 81:10).

God promises that if we seek Him, He will fill our mouths with the words we need to say.

If you have decided to ask Jesus into your heart, He is in you now and you in Him. May the God of hope fill you with joy and peace. Believe that He loves you and understands you completely.

Come to God with a teachable spirit, for He communicates through his Spirit to yours and through his Word. It's only by God's Holy Spirit that you can and will be changed into His glory. You are fearfully and wonderfully made for such a time as this.

My greatest prayer is that for the salvation of others, for broken hearts and wounded souls to be healed in Jesus Name. He loves you so much. What He has done for me, He will do for you. I pray God's favor to you that you will want to be set free to love God and everyone else. It is real!

God and I have a love affair. I love God with all my heart. I knew I was a new person when I was born again. Everything was bright, and I love my family so much. Never had I felt this way. I loved going to that first church and could not wait to hear what God had to say. The pastor was so full of love and let us all know how much God loved us.

The church had lots of singing guests and guest speakers. It is so exciting to watch and to see just how real God is. Thank God for the foundation I received upon becoming a new Christian.

I can remember when I was first born again; I would take my boys to school and could not wait to return home to read the Bible. I wanted everything God said I could have. I just believed in the Bible. Every word was like Jesus teaching and talking to me. I was so in love with Jesus and still am.

I remember reading and seeing Jesus and the disciples walking and could almost smell the dust. The Bible was so full of life and made me so happy. I felt God's presence when I would read and talk to Him. I love Jesus so much!

God has done so much for my thoughts, heart, and mind upon becoming born again and because God's Spirit came on me, I can say I have not been the same. It's almost as if He is reading to me as I cry. I have such a desire for God's Word to become alive in me because I love the Word of God and want to ask people if they know Jesus. I feel what I read, and I pray that you experience the same love.

It has been years since I was born again, but it just gets better and better every day with the Lord in my life. God says if we stay close to Him, He will guide us along today's journey. We have to enjoy today, right now, and not worry about what is around the corner. Concentrate on enjoying life right now. We are on the path God has chosen for us right this moment. Rest in Jesus and trust Him for everything. He is our tomorrow; we can rest in knowing that.

When I was first born again, I prayed a lot, and when I prayed in the spirit, it was as though I was sitting at Jesus' feet. I felt his presence. I would see, and I would hear things that would make me so happy. Then after the conversation or visit with Jesus, I would not be able to describe what I heard or saw, but it was the greatest thing.

Afterward, for hours or days, I felt differently. Nothing bothered me, just peace and joy were with me. I have experienced this many times in my life.

"To those who are open to My teaching, more understanding will be given." (Mark 4: 25a). We have to decide to start reading the Bible today. I know that when I picked up the Bible for the first time, God gave me such a hunger to know Him. How else do we find out who our creator is? The Bible is full of life. I pray that the anointing of the Holy Ghost will also cause you to want to draw close to Him.

God does speak to us; we have to know his voice. The Bible is a teaching manual to know Jesus and all He has for us. When we do not have a lot of stuff in our head, it becomes easy to read the Word of God and to believe it. "As Your words are taught, they give light, and even the simple can understand them." (Psalms 119:130).

After becoming born again, I have developed a holy boldness in me. I genuinely feel I can be me. I am not out to please anyone but Jesus Christ. He says He will even make my enemy silent. I have desired to speak the truth and not to be afraid of what someone may think of me. I am no longer a people pleaser.

"For I speak the truth and hate every kind of deception. My advice is wholesome and good. There is nothing crooked or twisted in it. My words are plain to anyone with understanding, apparent to those who want to learn." (Proverbs 8:7-9).

Begin to desire to speak the truth of God's word into yourself and know that His Word is life to you.

"Leave your foolish ways behind and begin to live; learn how to be wise." (Proverbs 9:6). The book of Proverbs teaches us how to live and how to have an abundance from each word of wisdom written there. Oh God, that we as your children will hunger for the real things of this time here in life. "Getting wisdom is the most important thing you can do. And whatever else you do, get good judgment." (Proverbs 4:7).

Sick people without hope will receive hope. People will receive God's love like never before. They will receive joy, peace, and understanding of God and his Word. They will receive healing and deliverance, and people will be set free from abuse.

There is hope. There is hope for children. There is hope for finances. There is hope for friendships. There is hope for mates. There is hope that you will come out of darkness into the marvelous light of Jesus Christ.

Hope is something positive we have had since childhood. But the kind of hope I had was that my dad would not make me stay awake at night for him, that he would not treat me the way he did. I was always hoping my life would be different.

Then while living in the children's home, I just hoped my father would not come to visit because I knew what he would do to me even in the home. He would sneak in to do things to me, all the while I was hoping someday, he would never touch me again.

In the meantime, I was hoping to get married and have someone protect me from my father. This hope became realized. I thank God for the wonderful man who later became my husband and who made sure my father could not come around after we were married.

My husband is a blessing to me. Even though we married at a young age, we have stayed married for more than 54 years. We started our life together with very little. My husband, being such a hard worker, has always been a consistent provider, protector and a proud father of our two sons.

I have been blessed. And, blessings continue coming to my family and me.

Hope comes from reading His beautiful letter to us, the Bible, saying take heart because we have peace in Jesus. "I have told you all this so that you may have peace in Me. Here on earth, you will have many trials and sorrows, but take heart because I have overcome the world." (John 16:33).

I know you may be in the middle of trials and sorrows. I speak peace over you and pray that you draw peace from Jesus. He says to come to Him when you are hurting, and He will take your pain. Let go of cares while Jesus changes your heart and your mind. Let go of worries and receive the peace that Jesus freely gives.

Take time to hear His voice, and that is primarily through the Word of God. The book of Proverbs is terrific for growing and knowing who we are and who our Savior is.

"In the same way, wisdom is sweet to your soul. If you find it, he will have a bright future, and your hopes will not be cut short." (Proverbs 24:14). When you have been disappointed, praise God, for these words are of a bright future. There is always hope.

One day while just thinking, I considered how most people have big baby pictures of themselves. Most people also have a birth certificate which in turn help them acquire other legal documents in life, such as a visa to travel to foreign countries. But I have none of these things.

These people also have childhood memories. I do not have a single remembrance of a Christmas celebration or any other holiday of any kind. I have no special childhood memories to reflect on. I listen to friends tell about trips that their family went on when they were children or some exceptional gift they received for just being the parent's child. So, as I am thinking about this, I cry. The reason I'm crying is I believe in my heart that is why I have such a special walk with my heavenly Father.

Maybe I have no memories; perhaps I have no pictures, but I know without a doubt, my picture is in the palm of Jesus's hand. And every time He looks at His hands, He sees me. Never to be forgotten. Never to be forsaken. Pictures fade and pictures get lost, but I know that my heavenly Father carries my picture with Him everywhere. Never to be forgotten, praise the Lord.

"As for me, I am poor and needy, but the Lord is thinking about me right now. You are my helper and my savior. Do not delay, oh my God." (Psalms 40:17). The Lord is thinking of me right now, and the Holy Spirit said that He was the greatest gift I could ever receive. What a blessing to hear this from God.

The Holy Spirit is so in love with us. Different people are telling how they are praying more and more and spending time reading their Bibles. It seems like God is showing up big in their lives. Changes are happening. Like people rising and praying in public, talking about miracles in their lives, or testimonies of family and friends. It is an awareness that everyone is now talking openly about God. God is getting the praise He so deserves.

I can speak for myself. From the moment of being born again, I have always loved Jesus. I could always talk about the things of the Lord with my friends. Even now, it is as natural as breathing for me to speak to people. I say, "Look what God is doing in my life."

With freedom, there is so much joy. Excitement is meant to be shared and not be hidden because I was ashamed or afraid; I would lose a friend.

I see things changing so fast in the news. What a great thing it is to tell someone there is a God who will help them during this time of trial and tribulation in our country. It is so easy to ask them to call on Jesus to save them, and he will be their counselor.

Several years ago, a friend from a church in Texas called and said God told her that Acts

26:16-18 was for me and that I would be speaking someday.

My "someday" is here now. Glory to God. "Arise, stand up on your feet: for I have appeared unto you for this purpose. To make thee a minister and a witness both of things we should have seen, and of those things in which thou hast seen, and of those things in the which I will appear unto thee; delivering thee from people, and from the Gentiles, unto whom now I send thee, to open their eyes, and to turn them from darkness to light, and the power of Satan unto God, that they may receive forgiveness of sins, and inheritance among them which are sanctified by faith that is in me." (See Acts 26:16).

I have also learned when we pray about something; we have to believe God's Word no matter what. I have found in many years as a Christian; sometimes it will take years to see things come to pass. Trust and believe! Without faith, it is impossible to believe.

It can be a slow walk when we are born again, but I am so excited to have come from a horrible life and then to know that I am just as clean as the apostles Peter, John, Mark, and even Jesus Himself. It's very exciting that God makes this so simple to the simple people. So thankful I was reading and believing.

Jesus Christ is God's love gift to the world (John 3:16), and believers are the Father's love gift to Jesus Christ. It is Christ who commits the believer to the Father for safekeeping so that the believer's security rest upon the Father's faithfulness to his Son Jesus Christ.

"The Spirit of the Lord is upon me, for He hath anointed me to preach Good News to the poor. He has sent me to proclaim that captives will be released, that the blind will see, that the downtrodden will be freed from their oppressors, and that the time of the Lord's favor has come." (Luke 4:18-19).

One time while talking to the Father and praising Him for my life, He said to my heart, "Suffering is but a fleeting moment." I can honestly say I thank God for all I've been through. That suffering now seems fleeting compared to what I currently have.

I love my walk with God more than life. I see how all the Word comes alive after reading and studying it for years. My heart is so full of God and his love.

For years I have written things down. Things I felt the Holy Spirit was saying to me. They were love letters from Him. I wasn't just thinking about these things. It was the lover of my soul speaking to me. Without a doubt I know it was God speaking.

"Be silent and know that I am God. Every nation will honor me. I will be honored throughout the world." (Psalm 46:10). He would speak to my heart with His Word, and I would write it on paper, along with the dates and times.

"My sheep recognize my voice; I know them, and they follow me." (John 10:27). I believe that

He speaks to those who have ears to hear. All these beautiful words from my heavenly Father has changed my heart.

I know we can't obey feelings, but my heart and thoughts have lined up with what God says. The Word of God is wonderful, and He helps daily with the things ahead. The Holy Spirit does speak to us.

Many, many times I have taken my needs to my Father. "You will live in joy and be led forth in peace. The mountains and Hills will burst into song, and the trees of the field will clap their hands." (Isaiah 55:12). We will go out with joy and be led forth in peace. That is where our strength comes from, not from things or people.

About ten years ago, a friend from another state came to visit me for the weekend. Our first night together, she was sharing her testimony and that of her husbands. I had never heard anything like it. I even got up and got a towel because I was crying so hard. God had done such healing in both her and her husband's lives from years of heartaches. I went to bed that night with such joy and peace.

The next night the same friend and I were talking again about the same things. However, I noticed this time was different; now her tone was angry. The first night she had been praising her husband, the second night she was filled with rage about him.

While stunned at her change in tone of voice, I looked up, and in the spirit, I saw Satan in the corner of the room giving orders to a demon to go to her husband and torment him during the night. Because of my friend's angry words towards her husband, I saw a demon spirit just ready to shoot out the door at Satan's command. We learned a great lesson that night.

"Death and life are in the power of the tongue: and they that love it shall eat the fruit thereof." (Proverbs 18:21 KJV).

I have been crying so much since I have come into this new level I am now in. One night I was crying while praying and talking to Jesus. Cry, cry, cry. I cry when I'm happy; I cry when I pray. I asked God one time what I was doing, why all the crying. He told me He bottles every tear I cried. And everyone else's for that matter. He has every tear that ever fell from our eyes. Then He showed me large rain barrels. One after another lined up. I laughed!

Another time I ask Him again why the crying. I happen to have my TV on a Christian broadcasting channel. A pastor that was speaking at that particular moment said that someone was crying a lot and that it was a language only God understood. So, let my tears come, Lord Jesus. I will never be ashamed of my tears. There were so many years I could not cry. Now, I cry freely. But then, my name fits me to a T. Dana Crier.

PART THREE
INSPIRATIONS FROM GOD

"Your Word is a Lamp Unto My Feet and a Light to my Path." (Psalms119:105).

We are so blessed to have a God that listens to our heart. It is the greatest feeling to be able to talk to Him anytime about everything. And that is why we have the joy of the Lord. Our trust is in our Father God!

"He made their hearts, so He understands everything they do." (Psalms 33:15).

"Taste and see that the Lord is good. O the joys of those who trust in Him." (Psalms 34:8).

"I rise early before the sun is up; I cry out for help and put my hope in your words. I stay awake through the night, thinking about your promise." (Psalms 119:147-148).

We are unique in our heavenly Daddy's eyes. He has a living word for us to follow and he has given us hearts to understand. We ask for help. Our help is in the Word. God's promises are true. Get into his Word to live a victorious life. God has revealed to us the truth there.

"And now, just as you accepted Christ Jesus as your Lord, you must continue to live in obedience to Him. Let your roots grow down deep into Him and draw up nourishment from Him so you will grow in faith, strong and vigorous in the truth you were taught, let your lives overflow with thanksgiving for all He has done." (Colossians 2:6-7). This is the new life in Christ.

"May God our Father give you grace and peace." (Colossians 1:2b).

"Surely goodness and mercy shall follow me all the days of my life: and I will dwell in the house of the Lord forever." (Psalms 23:6 KJV).

God, thank you for your Word. We pray to live holy as you are in our lives. We want to be just like Jesus and have a home like our own home above.

We want to be holy in our conversations and attitudes. Just like packing our suitcase for a trip, we want clean things in the suitcase (our heart). We want pure and holy thoughts there.

"So, set yourselves apart to be holy, for I, the Lord am your God. Keep all my laws and obey them, for I am the Lord, who makes you holy." (Leviticus 20:7-8).

God is Holy! What is holy? Consecrated and set aside for sacred use; standing apart from sin and evil.

God loves us so much, and we need His truth, which is the Word of God that sets us free. We become free by reading the Word and agree with it. We obey God's Word and sin will not entice us. If we do have sins, we can boldly enter into God's presence and receive forgiveness by confessing those sins. Confess means to admit or acknowledge our sin. Then, do not carry around the weight of those sins after confessing to God. He said He never remembers them again. It is a new lease on life.

It is so good to confess our sins because then God refreshes us in His presence. There is nothing like knowing the refreshment from our heavenly Father. "But if we confess our sins to Him, He is faithful and just to forgive us and to cleanse us from every wrong." (1st John 1:9).

For instance, when our children did something wrong, we knew it. We got them to talk about it. Sometimes they would be crying about it because of the fear of punishment. We spoke to them, and then once they confessed it moved on. At that point, we could not even remember what they did.

That is like our heavenly Father in heaven. He loves us so much that He remembers it no more. And nothing can separate us from God's love.

What can we say about such wonderful things as these? If God is for us, who can ever be against us? Who dares accuse us whom God has chosen for his own? Will God? No! He is the one who has given right standing with Himself. Who then will condemn us? Will Jesus Christ?

No, for He is the one who died for us and was raised to life for us and is sitting at the place of highest honor next to God, pleading for us. Can anything ever separate us from Christ's love? Does it mean He no longer loves us if we have trouble or calamity or are persecuted or are hungry or cold or in danger or threatened with death? (Romans 8:31,33-35).

"But I say, love your enemies! Pray for those who persecute you." (Matthew 5:44). Make your life easier by letting go! God will promote you, but not if you are angry, offended, or holding on to the past. Let it go!

God will help us that have been harmed or hurt. He will use this to make us stronger and use us for his glory. Trust and obey the Word and see what God can do for you.

God is so good! I would not change anything I've been through because I know my walk with God is so beautiful. God loves us so much!

Simply believe! Choose to believe what you read in the Bible! Prayer time is so important. When God speaks to us, love comes. Learn to love being with Him. There is nothing like it!

"Jesus loves us so much that His arms are open at all times. If we would just run to Him when we know, we have done wrong. Don't you realize that whatever you choose to obey becomes your master?" (Romans 6:16).

"But you belong to God, my dear children. You have already won the fight with these false prophets because the Spirit who lives in you is greater than the spirit who lives in the world." (1ˢᵗ John 4:4).

Even though we live in a nation that is taking God out of everything it can, such as the

"In God, we trust" on our money. Prayer being removed from our schools. Marriage vows broken.

We still have and always will have the freedom to walk with and obey God.

Sometimes after reading the Word of God and praying about a scripture over and over, we will be tested. For instance, we might be tempted to think about things that we know we should not.

But still, the most important thing we can do is read and pray every day to understand and speak the Word of God.

Spending time in the Word of God will get us to the point where thinking of something we shouldn't bother our conscious. That is because God corrects us with his Word.

If we expect to hear from God, we have to listen to His voice, and we can hear from Him by reading His Word.

God will put people in our lives that will speak the truth over us. For instance, I was doing something that I knew I shouldn't, and the Holy Spirit dealt with me about it. I happened to be outside watering plants one day when a friend I hadn't seen in years drove by looking for my house.

She realized she found me and stopped to give me a Word from God in an area that she had no idea I had been struggling with. She gave me scriptures which I knew came from God. I received that and wanted to make the necessary changes in my life.

But it can be hard to obey the Word of God when it convicts us of wrongs. The first thing that happens is that Satan tries to put guilt and shame on us in the areas where we don't pray or confess our faults. Then slowly we are not praying or reading the Word at all, which causes us to slip slowly away from the truth. But God corrects his children, often with His Word, to help us come back to Him.

Everything that is now hidden or see-through will eventually be brought to light.

Anyone willing to hear should listen and understand. And be sure to pay attention to what you hear. The more you do this, the more you will appreciate the Bible.

"For He hath said, I will never leave thee nor forsake thee." (Hebrews 13:5).

"The Lord will not abandon His chosen people, for that would dishonor His great name. He made you an exceptional nation for Himself." (1st Samuel 12:22).

"Even if my father and my mother abandon me, the Lord will hold me close." (Psalms 27:10).

"No, I will not abandon you as orphans; I will come to you." (1st John 14:8).

After you have received Christ as your Savior, know that He will take the place of all those things stolen from you. Jesus says He is the abundance! Every need and care we have is where He wants to bless us with His peace and love.

Our desires for things of God and to trust Him for everything in our lives will grow as we grow in Him. He has His everlasting arms around us at all times. Relax and enjoy God's presence now in the present. Trust this; you will never be the same once you entirely give your heart to Jesus Christ!

Rest in his presence when you need refreshment. Start reading the Bible, and you will find a fresh word for every need you have. Be conscious of God and start thanking Him for all His blessings, His love, His protection, His provisions. This requires time alone with Him. Relax. "Be still and know that He is God! Be still and know that I am God." (Psalms 46:10 KJV).

"For he hath said, I will never leave thee, nor forsake thee." (Hebrews 13:5b KJV). Just think about someone never leaving you. Never means not ever, at no time, not under any condition. Never leave means never to go away from, depart, desert, abandon, withdraw from. Never forsake means never to withdraw from or abandon.

What a comforting word from God Himself to us His children. He will never leave us at any time, under any condition, even during surgery or watching TV or driving around with friends or playing sports. He will never abandon us. God is with us while we are sleeping and waking up. He is with us every morning and throughout our day. That is why it is so powerful to talk with the Lord when we wake up.

Take time to be quiet and listen to Him talk about His written word. Let Jesus direct your thoughts towards Him. That is also why it's so important to know the promises of the Bible. Repeat what you know you should do, the ten commandments, for example, the Lord's prayer. See Matthew 6:9-13. Always aim at love. God is love and says so much about love in the Bible.

We can also pray for God's help anytime. Pray with the psalmist. "I am determined not to sin in what I say." (Psalms 17:3b). But if we do say something wrong, God's Word rises within us, and we can correct it right then, not letting it take our joy.

As your words are taught, they give light; even the simple can understand them. "Guide my steps by your Word, so I will not be overcome by any evil." (Psalms 119:130,133).

God is with you and watches over you wherever you go. The Lord is my strength, my shield from every danger. I trust Him with all my heart. He helps me; my heart is filled with joy; "I burst out in songs of thanksgiving." (Psalms 28:7).

God says, "Whenever you start to feel afraid, remember that I am your shield." His presence watches over you, continually protecting you from both known and unknown dangers. "God is our refuge and strength, always ready to help in times of trouble." (Psalms 46:1). The Lord watches over you.

"You know when I sit down or stand up. You know my every thought when far away. You chart the path ahead of me and tell me where to stop and rest. Every moment you know where I am." (Psalms 139:2-3).

If we would only get it into our hearts that God is with us, God gives peace. If only I had known this as a child or how important it was to teach this to my own children, instead of generations of curses, incest, and sickness. And to know that our heavenly Father knows everything about us is all the more reason to call on Him in times of trouble.

"Then Jesus said, come to Me, all of you who are weary and carry heavy burdens, and I will give you rest." (Matthew 11:28).

As we walk and grow in the Lord, we don't just get on the top of the mountain as fast as we think. Our walk with God has been fantastic, but sometimes we have had so much baggage and still seem to, that we keep learning and getting free of things that have held us down by reading and praying about those very things that still bother us.

Many people tell things they have been through, and burdens are the one word that always comes up. Burdens such as mothers or fathers who have guilt from spousal separations or divorce; mothers that have had abortions; fathers that have lost jobs; children that are drinking or doing drugs; someone very sick or has lost a loved one; hearts that carry so much pain.

Jesus says, "Come to Me when you are weak and weary." You can't continue getting help with drinking or doing drugs/pills. That alone will cause more problems. This is where you call on the name of Jesus. "He gives power to those who are tired and worn out; He offers strength to the weak." (Isaiah 40:29).

Jesus came so we could know God. For God so loved the world that he gave His only Son so that everyone who believes in Him will not perish but have eternal life." (John 3:16).

"For God sent not His son into the world to condemn the world: but that the world through Him might be saved." (John 3:17 KJV).

Who are we to condemn others? We don't want to condemn the people of this world. Just love people! Try and see them through the Lord's eyes. He died for them!

"And then He told them, go into all the world and preach the good news to everyone, everywhere." (Mark 16:15).

Do we love the world or the things of the world? Not when the love of the Father is in us. Since God gave us His love, love is always in partnership. And God's greatest gift? Everlasting life or life lasting forever.

Does God's Spirit feel comfortable in my heart? As the Amplified Bible says, "May Christ through your faith dwell, settle down, abide, and make his permanent home in your hearts." (Ephesians 3:17).

"And I pray that Christ will be more and more at home in your hearts as you trust in Him. May your roots go down deep into the soil of God's marvelous love." (Ephesians 3:17).

Our thoughts, our words, our actions have to be a place that God's Spirit wants to be. Sometimes we may feel like God is so far away. It is because of talking negatively about someone or holding on to something that they did to us, but God says we cannot hold on to the past. When we let go of the past, God moves in to create our present.

Preaching the gospel is a divine work because it changes lives. People need the good news of the gospel. They need to be set free.

Preach the gospel! When the gospel is preached correctly, people hear it, and changes come. God said we are made in his image. People need to understand that the Word of God and the Holy Spirit will move them out of darkness into His marvelous light and deliverance will come.

"So as much as in me is, I am ready to preach the gospel to you for I am not ashamed of the gospel of Christ: for it is the power of God unto Salvation to every one that believeth; to the Jew first, and also to the Greek." (Romans 1:15, 16 KJV).

"Preach the Word of God. Be persistent, whether the time is favorable or not, patiently correct, rebuke, and encourage people with good teaching." (2nd Timothy 4:2).

"I have not been afraid to speak out, oh Lord as you well know. I have not kept this good news in my heart; I have talked about your faithfulness and saving power. I have told everyone the great assembly of your unfailing love and faithfulness." (Psalms 40:9, 10).

He awakens us every morning with blessings, and we get into His Word to find out what He has for us that day. The Bible is so full of benefits for us, our families and our friends. Praise the Lord; praise God our savior! "For each day He carries us in His arms." (Psalm 68:19).

"Also blessed be the Lord who daily loads us with benefits, even the God of our Salvation." (Psalm 68:19 KJV).

It is great to lie down and go over the Word of God that has been put into our hearts. Who can think of any reason why not to read God's letter to us and to find all the wonderful plans He has for us now knowing our future is with our Father God? We can read something new every day!

Jesus responded, "Didn't I tell you that you will see God's glory if you believe?" (1ˢᵗ John 5:40). We have to be able to hear God's voice when the storms come against us. And when sickness comes, we have to be able to speak against the illness. How can we speak to the mountain of storms if we do not have the Word of God to fight against it? We cannot!

We have to speak God's Word through every area of our lives, through everything that we deal with daily. There is a way out with the Word! For example, sickness: sickness will not end in death. "When Jesus heard that, He said, this sickness is not unto death, but for the glory of God, that the son of God might be glorified thereby." (John 11:4).

When we know God as our Father or as Daddy, that is real intimacy. We live in a fatherless generation. Children are growing up without a father. We feel no security if we are children without a father, but God comes to show us what a father is like.

"Jesus told them, I am the way, the truth, and the life, no one can come to the Father except through Me." (John 14:6).

We need to awaken to Father God. We need to know God as our Father! Father has all the power. People cannot go on without knowing how much God loves them.

No matter what is going on in your life, refuse to give up hope. We have trials and pains in our lives. When you are hurting, say you are healed. When your home is in a mess, say it is peaceful. "Listen to me! You can pray for anything, and if you believe, you will have it." (Mark 11:24).

"We praise God, the Father of our Lord Jesus Christ, who has blessed us with every spiritual blessing in the heavenly's because we belong to Christ." (Ephesians 1:3).

Some days we may not feel like there is a reason to be joyful. Maybe that was experienced recently. We may not know why something is happening, but we can do something about it. We can start praising God, not asking for joy but praising God, and before we know it, we can be joyful. Things will look brighter and feel better!

"Believe on the Lord Jesus, And you will be saved, along with your entire household." (Acts 16:31). When you read a particular scripture in the Bible like this that relates to a need you may have, write it down and believe it is yours.

"Store my commands in your heart, for they will give you a long and satisfying life." (Proverbs 3:2). God's Word is our life. There is not one thing that we will ever go through that God hasn't supplied a way out. We put his Word in us to fully understand what the answer is. Not only that, God has given abilities to each of us. "A spiritual gift is given to each of us as a means of helping the entire church." (1st Corinthians 12:7). Only believe!

Take time to enjoy! Keep your mind on one thing at a time. More and more does not make you happy, nor does trying to impress others.

Clean clutter out of your house; get rid of things if they are not being used. Keep what you love. Be grateful for what you have. If you do not decide to be happy, you will never be satisfied.

Don't worry about anything; instead, pray about everything. Tell God what you need and thank Him for all He has done. If you do this, you will experience God's peace, which is far more wonderful than the human mind can understand. "His peace will guard your hearts and minds as you live in Christ Jesus." (Philippians 4:6,7).

There is no more excellent way to know our Daddy God than to pray. Read the Word of God, think of a scripture for the day, and learn to pray around it. God loves our prayers.

When there is a room full of people, for instance at a church, where maybe hundreds of people are, it is just a blessing to know that God hears everyone.

But to know without a doubt He has listened to you as if you are the only one person talking to Him, how special is this! The God of all creation listens to you! To know you can come to God just the way you are right now is so special.

God is helping you to grow and to become everything He wants you to be in wellness and strength. No matter what condition you are in, he hears you! Know that you can have great peace in the midst of things going on around you. You can talk to Him anytime.

THE CELLAR

"Pray at all times and on every occasion with the Holy Spirit. Stay alert and be persistent in your prayers for all Christians everywhere." (Ephesians 6:18).

Love is probably the most used word in the Bible. Our first thought is, Jesus is love because it is so hard to have a problem with another person when you know what the Word says about love. When you are walking closely with the Father, Son, and Holy Ghost, you love everyone.

The number one reason to love is that the Bible says to. We can be tested so many times in this area of our life. "Jesus said "A new commandment I give unto you. That ye love one another, as I have loved you, that ye also love one another." (John 13:34 KJV). To me, that says it all! Also, these three things will endure. Faith, Hope, and Love.

1st Corinthians 13:4-8

When you are angry with someone, think about these things in Corinthians. It seems like this scripture would be our answer when we get upset!

"Love is patient and kind."

"Love is not jealous or boastful or proud or rude."

"Love does not demand its own way.

Love is not irritable, and it keeps no record of when it has been wronged."

"It is never glad about injustice but rejoices whenever the truth wins out."

"Love never gives up."

"Love never loses faith."

"Love is always hopeful."

"Love endures through every circumstance."

"And the greatest of these is love."

Sometimes it can take a long time to get over being mad at someone. That is when it is so important to know the Word of God and to have the Holy Spirit to speak to our hearts. The mind will try to convince us that we have every reason to be upset.

One thing we can know for sure. When we let anger come in, we lose our joy and our peace. We can think about being wronged morning, noon, and night. But when we allow the Word of God to come up in our hearts, we begin to speak out about love and forgiveness, then we would not be full of anger and would walk in love as the problem grows smaller.

When we pray, that is when the Holy Spirit will rise up with the Word, and we repent and see this person in a whole new light! It is incredible how anger clouds our minds, and we feel so dark with thoughts. Then when the light of the Word gets into our minds, we see entirely differently.

We can learn to cast down wrong thoughts or pictures that may come into our mind. We can learn to plead the blood of Jesus over those crazy thoughts. When fear gets in our thoughts: plead the blood of Jesus and see the blood on the person that needs forgiving.

When we have heard some news about something pertaining to us, it can be easy to be in our thoughts and not be sensitive to others. For instance, a bad report can cloud our minds and thoughts and cause us to do dumb things.

My point is that we must try hard not to jump to get angry when we see others do what we have done. We have no idea what report someone may have obtained.

Maybe they experienced a death in their family or of a friend. Perhaps they're sick themselves. We have got to have patience with others.

Let us try to remember how we have needed love and forgiveness.

Heaven is our next step. Love not the world. Stop loving this evil world and all that it offers you, for when you love the world, you show that you do not have the love of the Father in you. And this world is fading away, along with everything it craves. But if you do the will of God, you will live forever. (1ˢᵗ John 2:15, 17).

God is getting us ready for heaven as we're getting our hearts right by asking the Father to forgive us of things that we have done.

Desire above all to want your heart pure before you meet your heavenly daddy.

"Now may the God of peace make you holy in every way and may your whole spirit and soul and body be kept blameless until that day when our Lord Jesus Christ comes again. God, who calls you, is faithful; He will do this." (1ˢᵗ Thessalonians 5:23,24).

"Bless the Lord, Oh my soul: and all that is within me, bless His holy name. Bless the Lord, Oh my soul, and forget not all his benefits: who forgiveth all thine iniquities; who healeth all thy diseases." (Psalms 103:1-3 KJV).

We must tell ourselves never to forget the good things He does for us. I have been thinking about my salvation. How did I get here today forty-some years later? I can write and say God has done everything he said he would do!

I pray that you learn how to believe God's Word in every area of your life; God is our hope! He is the lover of our souls.

THE CELLAR

As the psalmist says, He forgives all our sins and heals all our diseases. I cannot count how many times since my birth into God's family that I have needed this verse. But I always had the Holy Spirit. He would tug at my heart to repent and move on. I would sometimes try so hard to do it my way but knowing what God would say I would stay in a miserable state until I called on Jesus for help.

"Our God is a God who saves! The sovereign Lord rescues us from death." (Psalms 68:20). Praise God who did not ignore my prayers and did not withdraw his unfailing love from me.

"Don't copy the behavior and customs of this world, but let God transform you into a new person by changing the way you think. Then you will know what God wants you to do, and you will know how good and pleasing His perfect will is in your life." (Romans 12:2).

This means we have been changed. We renew our minds with the Word of God. We read it and do it. Get an understanding of the Word. Want the will of God in your life? Our thinking must line up with God's Word. It will give us new thoughts.

Feelings cannot be the boss of us any longer. "Anyone who doesn't love Me will not do what I say. And remember, my words are not my own. This message is from the Father who sent Me." (John 14:24).

God heals! Just say, "I am healed!", And refuse to believe a bad report. Believe God!

I went through a time where I had been coughing for months and months. I finally sought medical help and was examined by three different doctors. My condition was such that lying down or sitting up, I coughed; talking on the phone became difficult because I coughed; even eating was a struggle because I coughed. I was embarrassed because I coughed all the time!

All through this though, I refused to walk in fear. This was the time when the Word of God had to be alive in my spirit.

Don't worry about anything; instead, pray about everything. Tell God what you need and thank Him for all He has done. If you do this, you will experience God's peace, which is far more wonderful than any human can understand.

"His peace will guard your hearts and minds as you live in Christ Jesus." (Philippians 4:6-7).

There it is clearly stated that we will experience God's peace when we choose not to worry. We can know without a doubt all is well. When going through a trial, we can hear the Holy Spirit say "Be still. Be silent and know that I am God." "Every nation will honor me, and I will be honored throughout the world." (Psalms 46:10).

I was then told a biopsy must be done on a suspicious spot the doctor saw on my lung and thought it was cancer. But down in my heart, I knew it was not anything.

While waiting for the doctor to call to set a biopsy appointment, I heard the Holy Spirit speak clearly to my heart, "be still!" The doctor did call later only to say the suspicious spot had shrunk. No biopsy needed!

God tells you He is with you even when three different doctors may give a wrong diagnosis. Now this means that no matter what the circumstances are like, everything will work out because God will never fail you or forsake you. Praise the Lord!

God speaks to our spirit. He leads us by His Spirit in us. Go to Him for directions. When God speaks to our hearts, we know to stop and listen and do. The quieter you become, the more you hear from Him.

"Fear not; no one will be able to stand their ground against you as long as you live, for I will be with you as I was with Moses. I will not fail you or abandon you." (Joshua 1:5).

It is a miracle how God by His spirit gives us such peace when we cry out to Him during the storms in life. Let us be quick not to sit and think about the thing we are going through. Let us get our Bibles and find the answer. Then speak the word until peace takes place where fear was.

I know that I know God has a good plan for you and me. We cannot run to someone to pray for us every time we have a trial. We have to learn to call on Jesus's name. He knows what is going to happen every minute of the day. Read

Philippians 4:6-7 about not worrying and tell God everything.

God's peace is so beautiful that these verses say we let God's peace take over our mind. What our minds think on has to be in line with what God says. Pray for the mind of Christ.

"For I am giving you good guidance. Don't turn away from my teaching." (Proverbs 4:2).

"The fear of the Lord prolongeth days: but the years of the wicked shall be shortened." (Proverbs 10:27 KJV).

"The fear of the Lord is the beginning of wisdom: and the knowledge of the holy is understanding. For by me thy days shall be multiplied, and the years of thy life shall be increased." (Proverbs 9:10,11 KJV).

The fear of the Lord means to hate all appearance of evil.

God owns all the silver and gold in the world. Not only that, we have to believe God owns everything and believe what we read when we have any questions. God's blessings are mine and yours! Let the Holy Spirit control our lives.

"Bring all the tithes into the storehouse so there will be enough food in my temple. If you do, says the Lord Almighty, I will open the windows of heaven for you. I will pour out a blessing so great you won't have enough room to take it in! Try it! Let me prove it to you!" (Malachi 3:10).

Why tithe? "You are under a curse, for your whole nation has been cheating me." (Malachi 3:9).

Our checkbook is a mirror of to whom we belong. Our first fruits belong to God before other things get paid. The tithe is ten percent of our income. God is in financial management! He gives us above and beyond what we can believe. Prosperity? So much so that God says, prove me in this, "And I will rebuke the devourer for your sakes." (Malachi 3:10,11 KJV).

"All we have has all been given by God. Don't store up treasures here on earth, where they can be eaten by moths and get rusty, and where thieves break in and steal. Store your treasures in heaven, where they will never become moth-eaten are rusty and where they will be safe from thieves.

Where ever your treasure is, there your heart and thoughts will also be." (Matthew 6:19-21).

What we lay up for ourselves will one day be gone. God is storing up what we give, and we will receive 100 percent back. Trust God!

One of the most significant times of my Christian life was when I was newly saved and attending a small church. Alters were open after every service. I would see God move in so many ways! I brought many requests to the altars and would cry there. I have seen many of those tearful prayers answered today. I love altars. I can lay all my burdens there and pray and know God hears me.

What has happened to the altars? "May Your will be done here on earth, just as it is in heaven." (Matthew 6:10b).

Believe for yourself that God is showering and giving so much more of His Spirit. That is what it means to be hungry for more of everything that God has for us. That hunger makes us want to spend more time with Jesus and to pray, which is to talk and listen to Him.

"God blesses you who are hungry now, for you will be satisfied." (Luke 6:21a). Once you have sat at the table with Jesus, you will never be satisfied with a little to eat.

Once you have sat at the big buffet table with all the fruits you can eat, then not eating will leave you yearning for that yummy taste again.

Desire to be satisfied with your soul being so full of Jesus and every good thing that comes from Him.

Jesus says come and dine now come and have some breakfast! Jesus said. "And no one dared ask Him if He was the Lord because they were sure of it." (John 21:12). The master has enough for all the needs of his servants.

We have to be hungry where we want more of Jesus, finding time to get away from being too busy with talking on the phone, shopping, or sometimes even from eating, to spend quality time reading the Word and talking to Him. He will and does speak to us. Even Jesus departed into a quiet place away from everyone and things. "The next morning Jesus awoke long before daybreak and went out alone in the wilderness to pray." (Mark 1:35).

If Jesus had to stop and pray, how much more have we to stop and pray?

Jesus said to pick up your cross and follow Him. The victory is yours through Jesus. Resist the devil, and he will flee from you. The truth is the word of God. You are a servant of Jesus Christ. You are the sheep, and he is the Shepherd.

"The Lord is my Shepherd; I shall not want." (Psalms 23:1). God is with you. You shall dwell with the Lord forever and ever! God will never leave you nor forsake you.

Reading the Bible for several years, we come across scriptures we have read many times over. Sometimes those scriptures jump into our hearts. For instance, "above all else, guard your heart, for it affects everything you do." (Proverbs 4:23).

That means from our hearts are the springs of life or the forces of life. What is essential for us from going to bed to waking up is the first thing we hear in our spirit is that we have to guard our hearts every day, sometimes several times a day.

"Pay attention, my child, to what I say. Listen carefully. Don't lose sight of my words. Let them penetrate deep within your heart for they bring life and radiant health to anyone who discovers their meaning." (Proverbs 4:20-22). Such a powerful word to us to get into our hearts and live by.

"My child listen to me and do as I say, and you will have a long, good life. I will teach you wisdom's ways and lead you in straight paths." (Proverbs 4:10-11).

Desire more than anything else to listen and do what God is telling you. God tells us if we do what he says and if we discover and let all his words penetrate deep within our hearts, we will have a life full of blessings and radiant health.

We sometimes have to spend time and just read these verses over and over to get hold of what the Holy Spirit is saying to us.

We can read scripture several times until we know that we know what God is saying to us. That is when we can fill up those springs of living water in our soul with life. We can do this every single day by standing on the Word.

Sometimes our hearts can get wounded so severely by what someone says or does to us; like when something comes at us, and we want to think and think about it, then talk about it regarding what someone has done or said.

That is the time we can stand in the midst of it and speak these words about guarding our heart. It just works. This causes us to be able to move forward and not be damaged by it. God wants us to grow and speak his Word for our lives.

We can also struggle with wanting to please people. We can learn not to have to please anyone but Jesus Christ. Desire to speak the truth and not be afraid of what someone would think or try to be a people pleaser.

THE CELLAR

Desire to speak the truth into yourself and know that God's Word is life for you. A Godly boldness will develop in you from reading the word of God over and over. Set your mind on the Word of God, not what the world says about you.

God says you will rise again. Just know this! We know God is in us. Great heroes will come forth. "Those who are wise will shine as bright as the sky. And those who turned many to righteousness will shine like stars forever." (Daniel 12:3).

We will rise to be mighty, free people. We can help free others and bring them hope. We can help others put their hands back into God's hand.

"Lord, my heart is not proud, nor my eyes haughty; nor do I involve myself in significant matters, or things too difficult for me. Surely I have calmed and quieted my soul; like a weaned child resting with his mother, my soul is like a weaned child within me composed and freed from discontent." (Psalms 131:1-2 AMP).

I lay my head on God's chest. I put on the full armor of Christ: the belt of truth, the shoes of peace, and the shield of faith to stop every fiery dart from the devil. (See Ephesians 6:14-17).

Take your limits off God and let God be God! Believe you will see God do great miracles in your family, finances, and bodies. If you believe, you will receive. "No eye hath seen, nor ear has heard, and no mind has imagined what

God has prepared for those who love Him." (1st Corinthians 2:9).

We have to speak the Word of God regardless of what is going on right now. We cannot take our eyes off the Word. Our ears have to hear what God says. We cannot be hearers only but must also be doers of the Word. Desire to be a doer of the Word. And remember, it is a message to obey, not just to listen to. If you don't obey you are only fooling yourself (James 1:22).

WISDOM IS LIFE TO US AS BELIEVERS

From the Book of Proverbs

- Makes us wise. (1:23)
- Peace and safety, being unafraid. (1:33)
- Understanding. (2:3)
- Knowledge of God. (2:5)
- A shield of protection.
- Right, just and fair.
- Joy.
- Keeps us from evil people.
- Loyalty and kindness.
- Favor with God and people.
- Good reputation.
- Renewed health and vitality. (3:8)
- Fills our barns.
- He corrects us (because He loves us).
- Happy. (3:13)
- Guidance.
- Tree of life.
- Honor and respect.
- Keep my feet from stumbling.
- Lie down without fear.
- Not afraid of disaster.

The book of Proverbs teaches us how to live and how to have an abundance from each word of wisdom written there. Oh God, that we your children will hunger for the real things of this time here in life.

"Wisdom is the principal thing; therefore, get wisdom: and with all thy getting, get understanding." (Proverbs 4:7).

The proverbs are so easy to read, but we've got to read over and over to understand what the Holy Spirit wants us to know about wisdom.

Many mothers, fathers, and children have pain: Children with divorced parents; parents on drugs; deaths in the family while young.

There are probably several people whom we know that we would not think could have horrific childhood pain.

My point here is that we as Christians have to have the compassion and love of Jesus in our hearts before we can help others and pray for them. We have to have the fruit of the spirit working in us at all times.

But when the Holy Spirit controls our lives, He will produce this kind of fruit in us: love, joy, peace, patience, kindness, goodness, faithfulness, gentleness, and self-control. Here there is no conflict with the law. (Galatians 5:22,23).

When we pray and ask God to teach us how to operate in this fruit daily, we will have more compassion for others.

Patience is another spiritual fruit we have to have. Getting mad or irritated at someone because traffic is too slow, or people are talking too much at the checkout line at the store when we are in a hurry. You know what I am talking about.

Plus, loving others is one spiritual fruit that is always coming up in our daily walk. The Bible says a lot about love and its importance, especially that God loves us all so much. He does know our pain, our heartaches. Jesus wants us to understand how to give our burdens to Him.

I know the Lord is always with me. I will not be shaken, for He is right beside me (Psalms 16:8). When we understand the love God has for us, we will receive his love and have the freedom of knowing who we are in Him.

Those who belong to Christ Jesus have nailed the passions and desires of their simple nature to His cross and crucified them there. If we are living now by the Holy Spirit, let us follow the Holy Spirit's leading in every part of our lives.

"Let us not become conceited or irritate one another or be jealous of one another." (Galatians 5:24-26).

Jesus says to trust Him in the depths of our being. When we settle down from being so busy with life and take the time to hear from God, our lives change in every area. "Be still and know that I am God." (Psalms 46:10a).

Slow down your pace of living for a while. Get into God's presence, and you will learn to hear his voice. He says to us, "Let me show you the way for this day." We are to relax and enjoy our lives and the presence of Jesus. He has so much to tell us. We have got to stop and listen.

God says when we pray, He will put his thoughts into our minds. We have the mind of Christ! "My child listen to me and do as I say, and you will have a long, good life." (Proverbs 4:10).

When we seek God, we can put aside thoughts and everything else. We can open our hearts and minds and receive from Him. Trust God! Life will be blessed when we hear God and believe what we read in the scriptures.

Commit everything you do to the Lord, Trust Him, and He will help you. Be still in the presence of the Lord and wait patiently for Him to act. Don't worry about evil people who prosper or fret about their wicked schemes. (Psalms 37:5,7)

We do not have to doubt that God will answer us. Talk to Him about everything. "But I will call on God, and the Lord will rescue me. Morning, noon, and night I plead out loud in my distress, and the Lord hears my voice. He rescues me and keeps me safe from the battle waged against me, even though many still opposed me." (Psalms 55:16-18).

Giving is one of the greatest blessings and giving time praying for others when they have a need. Taking a meal or a cake to someone can also be a blessing. A door can be opened to pray for the needs of others or to ask if they know Jesus Christ as their Savior. Being a blessing to someone is refreshing.

"Do not forget to show hospitality to strangers, for by so doing some people have shown hospitality to angels without knowing it." (Hebrews 13:2).

THE CELLAR

"Don't forget to do good and to share what you have with those in need for such sacrifices are very pleasing to God." (Hebrews 13:16).

"It is possible to give freely and become wealthier, but those who are stingy will lose everything." (Proverbs 11:24).

"The generous prosper and are satisfied; those who refresh others will themselves be restored." (Proverbs 12:25).

My mother in law told me a story I will never forget. She was cleaning the kitchen one morning when someone knocked on the door. She went to the door and saw a man who looked like a bum asking for something to eat. While she was preparing breakfast, he waited at the kitchen table. After the man ate, all at once it got quiet. She turned to see the man was no longer there! She never heard the door open or close. She looked outside, but the man was nowhere to be found. She always believed an Angel had visited her, which I think so, too!

Don't forget to show hospitality to strangers, for some who have done this have entertained Angels without realizing it! (Hebrews 13:2).

From The Book Of Hebrews

"For only we who believe can enter his place of rest." (4:3a).

"God's rest is there for people to enter." (4:6a).

"Today you must listen to his voice. Don't harden your hearts against Him." (4:7b).

"There is a special rest still waiting for the people of God." (4:9).

"Let us do our best to enter that place of rest." (4:11a).

"That is why we have a great High Priest who has gone to heaven, Jesus, the son of God. Let us cling to Him and never stop trusting Him." (4:14).

"This High Priest of ours understands our weaknesses." (4:15a).

"Let us come boldly to the throne of our gracious God. There we will receive his mercy, and we will find grace to help us when we need it." (4:16).

THE CELLAR

From The Book Of Philippians

"May God our Father and the Lord Jesus Christ give you grace and peace." (1:2).

"I pray that your love for each other will overflow more and more and that you will keep on growing in your knowledge and understanding." (1:9).

"God is working in you, giving you the desire to obey Him and the power to do what pleases Him." (2:13).

"In everything, you do stay away from complaining and arguing so that no one can speak a word of blame against you." (2:14-15).

God never gives up on us. Just like with our children, we never stop loving them. It can be so sad about what they're doing, but Jesus says he loves our children and us unconditionally.

God will give us another chance. Don't settle for less than God's best. Our God is so good and full of mercy, He says to our hearts not to be discouraged. He restores the years that have been stolen. Refresh us, Lord Jesus.

Be kind to those who hurt you. People do not always know what they're doing. Just like Job who lost everything, God restored his losses all back to him and more. (See Job 42).

Trust God!

"But I say love your enemies! Pray for those who persecute you." (Matthew 5:44).

When a friend comes to see you, and they are in pain or having some difficulty, don't lecture them. Listen to them. God will promote you if you forgive others. Become like a little child. Go on and do not hold bitterness or anger. Release it all to God. He will make it right!

Little children just believe! Dream a little. Create some joy in your life. Move into the supernatural realm. God is closer than you think! Stop being so mature and boring. Children believe. Don't doubt, only believe. It is a choice. Get out of the realm of your mind and follow God's Word. So many Christians are just mad. Let it go! Turn away from this.

"The commandments of the Lord are right, bringing joy to the heart. The commands of the Lord are clear, giving insight into life." (Psalms 19:8).

Trust in God's plan for your life and future. God has grand plans for you. Believe that what happens to you is for the best. God has only the best for you.

Have you ever prayed and prayed about something you wanted, and it just didn't happen? But later you saw God had something so much better in his plan for you. Do you take time and thank God when you see a door close, and a more excellent plan has worked out for you? God is in complete control of your life. He is God!

Cancel the wrong report. The words we speak are so powerful. Life and death are in the power of the tongue. Emotion cannot override what God says. When we dare to step out, our heavenly Father will not let us down! Believe and receive!

"A gossip betrays a confidence, but a trustworthy person keeps a secret." (Proverbs 11:13). Do not ever repeat what someone tells you in confidence.

Enjoy the journey. You cannot help everyone; Jesus died for you to enjoy life! Do not break the health rules by getting too busy. Do not put too much on your plate like going and going and not taking time for God or yourself. This will be a problem, and you will not be happy. Blaming everyone else is not the answer. If you are not satisfied, do something about it. Making wise choices makes us happy.

Stop, listen, and pray for wisdom. Wisdom chooses to do what is right now for what will benefit us later on. Our thoughts can change. We have control to move forward.

Want more of Jesus, the word, and the anointing? Wisdom is a must! "Cry out for insight and understanding. Search for them as you would for lost money or hidden treasure." (Proverbs 2:3).

For the Lord grants wisdom. "From His mouth come knowledge and understanding." (Proverbs 2:6).

"For wisdom will enter your heart, and knowledge will fill you with joy." (Proverbs 2:10).

Moses pleaded with the Lord; "Oh Lord I'm not a good speaker. I have never been, and I'm not now, even after you have spoken to me. I am clumsy with words".

"Who makes mouths?" The Lord asked him. "Who makes people so they can speak or not speak, hear or not hear, see or not see? Is it not I, the Lord?"

"Now go and do as I have told you. I will help you speak well, and I will tell you what to say." (Exodus 5:10-12).

"Open your mouth wide, and I will fill it with good things." (Psalms 81:10b).

God speaks to our hearts and prepares us to speak for Him. Stand on these verses before you talk to people or speak at a meeting. God knows what each listener needs to hear. Trust in Him to speak through you and let His Spirit speak to people's hearts. Salvation, healings, and deliverance come from God. Let Him fill your heart with his Word to speak for Him.

When we see Jesus, our desires change. The devil does not know anything about us. We tell him with our words. Are words should line up with God's promises. If we speak death, sickness, or lack it is the devil's language, and he sends his demons. Stop and say what God says. He gives his Angels charge over our words.

The devil hates for us to be blessed. We have to do spiritual warfare. If God is for us, who can be against us? Blessing and cursing should not come out of the same mouth. This is wrong! Life and death are in the power of the tongue. Our tongue can loose torments on others. We should bless them instead.

This is a good reason to pray in the spirit. We are talking to God in another language. He knows our thoughts and if we are angry or upset with someone, praying in the spirit releases God's anointing and love for someone we cannot love in our self. But God will cause a spirit of love to cover the sin that so easily besets us. Let God fill our thoughts and hearts with his love for others.

Be careful how you talk about yourself. You will never rise above your confession. What you say goes to the spiritual realm. Line up your mouth with the Word of God. Your fruit will be so good. Who are you to disrespect what God made? Get over it! Do not compare yourself with anyone. You are not weird; you are unique! Be careful how you talk about God.

"Then those who feared the Lord spoke with each other and the Lord listened to what they said. In His presence, a scroll of remembrance was written to record the names of those who feared Him and love to think about Him." (Malachi 3:16).

God is faithful! He is good to us.

Be careful how you talk about people. Do not fault people. Do not tell anything bad you know about others. Use self-control. Cover your friends. Three brothers were told the facts about their father; two covered him up. (See Genesis 9:20-27).

So, get rid of all malicious behavior and deceit. Don't just pretend to be good. Be done with hypocrisy, jealousy, and backstabbing. You must crave pure spiritual milk so that you can grow into the fullness of your salvation. "Cry out for this nourishment as a baby cries for milk, now that you have had a taste of the Lord's kindness." (1ˢᵗ Peter 2:1-2).

Don't grumble about each other my brothers or God will judge you. For look! The great Judge is coming. He is standing at the door (James 5:9). It is none of our business. It is between them and God.

"He replied, what is impossible from a human perspective is possible with God." (Luke 18:27).

"I can do everything with the help of Christ, who gives me the strength I need." (Philippians 4:13).

"May the grace of the Lord Jesus Christ be with your spirit." (Philippians 4:23).

Love to read the Word and to find scriptures. Jesus Christ knows every need we have and has a word for it. Say yes to the Word of Life and Truth. Let your roots grow down into Him and draw up nourishment from Him, so you will grow in faith, strong and vigorous in the truth you were taught. "Let your lives overflow with thanksgiving for all he has done." (Colossians 2:7).

You are entitled to these blessings. You are about to walk in your benefits. You can ask for rain blessings. The rain will loosen up some stuff in your life. Rain will wash you. You are entitled to God's blessings. I pray as you read this that you believe and receive your healing, forgiveness, and benefits that our Father has for you. You are a blessing to the ones around you.

"Give your burdens to the Lord, and He will take care of you. He will not permit the Godly to slip and fall." (Psalms 55:22).

God says we are His at all times. And when we get this in our heart, not one thing can stop us from receiving his protection.

Pray to give your cares and problems to Jesus. He will take them from you and give you such peace. This sounds almost too easy, but it requires a deep level of trust knowing God's way is perfect.

"I am leaving you with a gift — peace of mind and heart. And the peace I give isn't like the peace the world offers. So, don't be troubled or afraid." (John 14:27).

The enemy likes to steal your joy. So do not throw away this confident trust in the Lord, no matter what happens. Remember the great reward it brings you. Patient endurance is what you need now, so you will continue to do God's will. Then you will receive all that He has promised. (Hebrews 10:35-36).

Do not throw away your confidence. Keep your faith in the middle of a trial. Continue to declare what God has promised you. Your confidence has to stay high. It will give you victory when the enemy comes in to steal the word. God is the same regardless of what the devil does. God is still the same.

The word of God will be performed in your life. Lose confidence, and you lose your joy, praise, and promise. Keep your confidence active at all times and keep your heart right with God. Dear friends, if our conscience is clear, we can come to God with bold confidence. "And we will receive whatever we request because we obey Him and the things that please Him." (1ˢᵗ John 3:21-22).

There is a way that seems right to a man, but not with God. Walk in line with God's Word. The biggest problem we have is not speaking what the word of God says. The book of James says our mouth gets us in trouble. (See James 2:1-11).

Speaking the opposite of what God says, we lose everything. But speak the Word, and we will have all God promises us. We need to renew our minds. We cannot ask for a promise if we do not know the promises.

Expect great things from God. Cheer yourself up. Live with the holy expectancy. Be expecting good from God. Wealth. God's favor. What is favor? God's kindness and help to reward you, promotion, and supernatural increase. The earth does not govern heaven. Walk in God's favor. It causes people to go out of their way to bless you.

The favor of God is working in your life now, bestowing to you and your families.

"For the Lord is a sun and shield; the Lord bestows grace and favor and honor; no good thing will He withhold from those who walk uprightly." (Psalms 84:11).

Stop judging others, and you will not be judged. For others will treat you as you treat them. (See Matthew 7:1-2a).

Do for others what you would like them to do for you. This is a summary of all that is taught in the law and the prophets (Matthew 7: 12).

"But when you are praying, first forgive anyone you're holding a grudge against, so that your Father in heaven will forgive your sins, too." (Mark 11:2-5).

We have to be sure to forgive quickly. The quickest way to lose our joy is by holding a grudge. We can take a word someone has said and entirely turn it around from what it started out to be. Forgiving others has to be important to us because we want God to forgive us when we sin.

We grieve the Holy Spirit by holding on to something and not giving our problems, anger, our judgment to Him. He is our counselor. Go to God before we start talking to everyone about what someone has done to us.

"A fool is quick-tempered, but a wise person stays calm when insulted." (Proverbs 12:16). We all have been offended by someone, but we have to learn not to let those words get into our hearts. It is hard not to tell what someone has said about us. A story gets twisted when it starts traveling around.

When I was first born again, I wrote down all the scriptures I could find about gossiping, unforgiveness, grudges, and the like. I found out God is not pleased with our words when we repeat over and over what someone said about others or ourselves.

Forgiveness is not easy, but if we want to hear from God, we have to forgive, to let it go fast. Words fester and cause sickness to our souls. We must take personal responsibility for what we do with what we hear.

I have learned from a dear friend that when gossiping starts, ask "Were you there to witness this?" Generally, the answer is no, but in any case, learn not to listen to the gossip. Get up and leave the conversation.

Let's desire to be like the wise woman in the book of Proverbs. "She opens her mouth with wisdom and in her tongue is the law of kindness." (Proverbs 31:26 KJV).

Do not let unexpected events throw you off course. Instead respond calmly and confidently, remembering that God is with you. As soon as something grabs your attention, talk to God about it. Thus, He shares your joys and your problems; He helps you through whatever is before you. This is how He lives in you and works through you. This is the way of peace.

"They do not fear bad news; they confidently trust the Lord to care for them."

(Psalms 112:7). "Don't be afraid for I am with you, do not be dismayed for I am your God. I will strengthen you. I will help you. I will uphold you with my victorious right hand." (Isaiah 41:10).

"God has called us. God hears the humble in heart. Be humble and gentle. Be patient with each other, making allowance for each other's faults because of your love. Always keep yourself united in the Holy Spirit and bind yourself together with peace." (Ephesians 4:2-3).

In the same way, you wives must accept the authority of your husbands, even those who refuse to accept the good news. Your Godly lives will speak to them better than any words. They will be won over by watching your pure, Godly behavior. "You should be known for the beauty that comes from within, the unfading beauty of a gentle and quiet spirit, which is so precious to God." (1ˢᵗ Peter 3:1,2,4).

Be able to give to another; then you will be strengthened. Give the advantage, not take it. If you are spiritually broke, you are needy. Needy people scare people. It is too much drama. Boldness is to be shared with someone else. Minister to others your boldness, releasing something to someone else.

We cannot do one thing without God's anointing. Not walking in love is the only thing that keeps us from the anointing. If we get away from the truth, we have to repent and ask forgiveness first. Believe in the power of prayer.

Keeping our hearts and minds on Jesus gives us the anointing. We can pray for someone, give them a word, or talk to Jesus for ourselves.

Was I born like this? "For I was born a sinner. Yes, from the moment my mother conceived me." (Psalms 51:5).

We all have the same right to choose to change. Our job is to help people. Life or death is everyone's choice. True freedom is accepting Jesus. Even though sin is passed down through generations, the good news is the blood of Jesus makes us free to walk away from the sin.

God has put something in us to make us strong. We have a heavenly daddy that has given us so much strength to go through trials, pain, or sickness. We have just got to stand on His Word. We cannot receive a bad report. Believe only what God says about us. We must get his Word in our hearts. If God is for us, who can be against us? We are the head and not the tail, above and not below.

Know that Jesus Christ is the rock of your Salvation. Think of a rock to hide under when you have to pray or intercede. Know the solid rock will never move. It is always there for you. "The Lord continued; stand here on this rock beside me. As my glorious presence passes by, I will put you in the cleft of the rock and cover you with my hand until I have passed by." (Exodus 33:21-22).

There may be many times you have to go to the cleft of the rock to cry when you need to pray. No one is holy like the Lord. "There is no one besides you; there is no rock like our God." (1ˢᵗ Samuel 2:2).

"The Lord is my rock, my fortress, and my Savior; my God is my rock, in whom I find protection. He is my shield, the strength of my Salvation, and my stronghold." (Psalms 18:2).

A stronghold is a fortified place, place of security or survival.

You sometimes need protection against your mind when you get a report of sickness or disease. But the report can change. No, despite all these things, overwhelming victory is ours through Christ who loved us (Romans 8:37).

The doctor may come out after surgery and say that there is cancer. But the report can change. If God is for you, who can be against you?

Jesus Christ loves you so much. He will never change. He is your solid foundation. Seek the Lord, and His strength, seek His face evermore. (Psalms 105:4).

Jesus says to His children, trust Me with your life. I have a good plan for you. Don't walk in fear or doubt. Just put your trust in Jesus and watch Him make your crooked path straight. Trust Jesus!

"God, I believe your heart has shown me the seriousness of talking about someone. God, I pray that my heart will be pure and holy until I see you in heaven. God, you mean business with your Word; I want to retain what I read and know what is right at this hour. I do not want to hurt anyone or repeat what I hear about anyone. I believe that it is so wrong to repeat what I hear about others. The story probably has no truth to it.

Please God, let me know in my heart when I sin with my mouth or thoughts. I don't want to be in a conversation and agree with anyone talking about someone. Help me to be like Jesus. Amen."

"Let me live so I can praise you, and may your laws sustain me." (Psalm 119:175). "I have hidden your word in my heart, that I might not sin against you." (Psalms 119:11).

Nothing would be available to us without the blood of Jesus. We know who we are because of the blood of Jesus. We are delivered from the opinions of people. We are blood Christians and can plead the blood daily over ourselves, our family, and our friends.

Know your rights by the blood. Know about the blood. Believe in the blood. Appropriate the power of the blood by faith. Receive your healed marriage by the blood of Jesus, see your children restored, receive your victory, get bills paid, children's bills paid.

God is our only source. Trust Him only. God is our one source. Things could get worse. But trust God. Rise out of the Ashes. Rise out of trouble. Let go. Plead the blood over everything. Expect a miracle. This is your day!

For you know that God paid a ransom to save you from the empty life you inherited from your ancestors. And the payment He paid was not mere gold or silver. He paid for you with the precious lifeblood of Christ, the sinless, spotless Lamb Of God. (1st Peter 1:18-19).

The blood is precious when you have lacked. It redeems, it delivers from the devil and the power of darkness. Jesus paid the price with his blood. We are delivered from the power of darkness by the blood.

The blood has purchased our redemption and inheritance. We are always thanking the Father, who has enabled you to share the inheritance that belongs to God's holy people, who live in the light. For He has rescued us from the one who rules in the Kingdom of darkness, and He has brought us into the Kingdom of His dear son. God has purchased our freedom with His blood and has forgiven all our sins. (Colossians 1:12-14).

The blood of Jesus ensures that Satan has no more power over us. Forgiveness of sin is ours by the blood. There is nothing so bad that Jesus has not washed it away. God wants to walk with us. There is no more guilt.

Let no one accuse you of anything. We are no more a slave to darkness. So, if the son sets you free, you will indeed be free. (John 8:36). Free indeed. Freedom has come to us. We are forever free by the blood of Jesus.

We can have our ways, our plans, and desires. We can hide our heart from people, but not from God. He sees and hears everything we do. There are no secrets from God. We cannot escape from God's love. And because of His great love for us, we can confess our wrongs and be forgiven. Stand still and see the glory of God.

Are you afraid of the dark? God is there. Are you fearful of enemies? God can take care of them.

Our God is an awesome God. Do you have fear because the path before you is full of danger? You serve a God that will answer you. No good thing will He withhold from you, and He will not leave you nor forsake you. He is a friend that sticks closer than a brother.

This is a new day! Seek the Kingdom of God. Coming around the corner, something is about to happen. You can now hear things differently. So, seek first the Kingdom of God and His righteousness. Believe you receive precisely what God has for you. The Holy Spirit will show you things to come.

God is light. "This is the message He has given us to announce to you: God is light, and there is no darkness in Him at all." (John 1:5). Your faith will be energized if you walk in the light you have. God is light. Light means to do what you know is right. In God's grace and mercy, he cleanses you when you repent.

Do not judge someone else because you do not know how much of the light has been given to another. Do not criticize. Dear friends, if our conscience is clear, we can come to God with bold confidence.

"And we will receive whatever we request because we obey Him and do things that please Him." (1st John 3:21-22).

PART FOUR
SEVEN STEPS TO RECEIVE EMOTIONAL HEALING

"Bless the Lord, Oh my soul and forget not all his benefits; Who forgiveth all thine iniquities; Who healeth all thy diseases; Who redeemeth thy life from destruction; Who crowneth thee with loving kindness and tender mercies." (Psalms 103:2-4).

1. Ask Jesus Christ into your heart
"For God so loved the world that He gave His only Son so that everyone who believes in Him will not perish but have eternal life." (John 3:16).

2. Cast your cares on Him
After receiving Jesus into your heart, you will be different! Cares will lift off you!

"Therefore, if any man be in Christ, he is a new creature: old things are passed away, behold, all things have become new." (2nd Corinthians 5:17 KJV).
What this means is that those who become Christians, become new persons. They are not the same inside anymore, for the old life is gone. "A new life has begun." (2nd Corinthians 5:17).

3. Become hungry for the Word of God
"Thy words were found, and I did eat them; and thy word was unto me the joy and rejoicing of mine heart: for I am called by thy name, O Lord God of host." (Jeremiah 15:16 KJV).
All scripture is inspired by God and is useful to teach us what is right and to make us realize what is wrong in our lives. It straightens us out and shows us to do what is right. It is God's way of preparing us in every way, thoroughly equipped for every good thing God wants us to do. (2nd Timothy 3:16-17).

4. Become willing to follow wherever God leads
God orders our steps daily. You will have doors open to you to speak life into others. "Go to now, ye that say today or tomorrow we will go into such a city, and continue there a year, and buy and sell, and get gain: whereas you know not what shall be on the morrow. For what is your life? It is even a vapor, that appeareth for a little time, and

then vanisheth away. For that ye ought to say, if the Lord will, we shall live, and do this, or that." (James 4:13-15 KJV).
"The Lord directs the steps of the Godly. He delights in every detail of their lives." (Psalms 37:23).

5. **Seek wisdom**
Choose life and blessing.
"For the Lord giveth wisdom: out of his mouth cometh knowledge and understanding. He layeth up sound wisdom for the righteous: he is a buckler or shield to them that walk uprightly." (Proverbs 2:6-7).
"Choose to love the Lord your God and to obey Him, and commit yourself to Him, for he is your life." (Deuteronomy 30:20a).

6. **Allow healing and miracles for your body**
God's word brings help and is like medicine to your flesh.
"My child pay attention to what I say. Listen carefully to my words. Don't lose sight of them. Let them penetrate deep into your heart, for they bring life to those who find them, and healing to their whole body." (Proverbs 4:20-22).

7. **Find your identity in God and thus have freedom with God**
Freedom is one of the greatest gifts that we can receive from our Father God. He takes broken vessels and makes them into the

children of God He so desires us to be. This freedom allows us to see ourselves as very special to Him, resulting in not being concerned about trying to please people. That is the greatest freedom. Relying on ourselves can lead to insecurities that among other things can cause us to want everyone to like us.

Learning to rely on God and knowing when to say no is such freedom. When we understand the love God has for us, we will receive His love and have the privilege of knowing who we are in Him.

Yes, we have to believe God's Word about everything in our lives, including our relationship with Him, what to do with our emotions, stress or sickness.

Concerning our emotions, our body picks up the messages that our emotions send. For instance, we think we can bury emotional pain so deep, but our body knows when we are holding onto it. We have to forgive others so we can be healed from the pains.

In my case, I spoke blessings over my parents even when my mind cried out not too, and I saw healings in my own body. God's Word is His way of doing things to set us free from the pain.

This comes from our relationship with Him. "Pay attention, my child, to what I say. Listen carefully. Don't lose sight of my words, let them penetrate deep within your heart, for they bring life and radiant health to anyone who discovers their meaning." (Proverbs 4:20-22).

When something bad happens, when fear comes, we tend to shut it up in our hearts, i. e. the bad things, the pain. But when someone offends us, Jesus says to forgive them.

We want to get even sometimes and talk negatively about them. However, remember God Forgives us of all of our trespasses. When we have something against someone, forgive them so that our Heavenly Father may forgive you.

God says we cannot get forgiveness for ourselves. We have to go to Him. We have to give all our offenses to God because unforgiveness blocks fellowship with Him.

This means that God must withhold from us many blessings that might otherwise come to us. We don't have to feel like forgiving. Forgiveness is not an emotion but a decision.

Jesus has the perfect plan for us. Don't try to figure it out, give your pains to Jesus; watch Him do what he said He would do for you.

For many years while growing up, I would bite my fingernails. I also had clutched fist holding on to pain and shame. But my hands are open now to receive blessings from my Father God.

God will hear you when you ask Him for help. Ask Him to give you the grace to forgive. You will and can do this. You will have the mind of Christ to understand His Word. You will be a blessing to someone.

God will use you to hear the pain of someone else, and you will pray for them for their healing. Praise God. He wants you to be free and bless others.

In the book of John, we are told to confess our sins, and God will forgive us. (See 1st John 1:9). Sometimes, we may feel we need to forgive God. We think he did something to us. Merely say, God, I forgive you. Don't blame God. At the cross Jesus forgave the people persecuting Him. Please forgive others today. Freedom is yours today.

Living in dependence on Jesus is the most magnificent abundant life we could ever ask for. God wants us to trust Him for everything. We can have freedom from pain, neglect, abuse, weakness, loneliness, or fear. But we have to watch how we respond to others.

Some of our problems can be and are rooted in us. We have to go before God and ask Him to show us if there is anything we need to deal with, sometimes things can upset us; sometimes, it is the truth that we have not dealt with.

When we see an issue that keeps coming up, the enemy does all he can to keep us in darkness. Pray and ask God to bring the light in order to get free from it. We want to be free from everything that is not Godly in us. God loves us and wants us to have the freedom to be who He wants us to be.

The good news is no matter how dismal our current situation or outlook, we are assured by God; this too shall pass.

Put on the full armor of God (See Ephesians 6:10-18). The enemy will attack us when we are weak and will try to run over us. He never stops telling us we will never amount to anything. He will tell us we are not as good looking as others or that we are sick. Or even a multitude of other wrong things.

Well, remember this, he is a liar. "The thief cometh not, but for to steal, kill and destroy. I come that they might have life and have it more abundantly." (John 10:10 KJV).

It is so important to find a Christian that knows how to pray. Pray for Kingdom friends that know how to plead the blood of Jesus over you. We have to know who's voice we are listening to. Is it Father God or the enemy? Jesus said a stranger's voice we will not follow.

The gatekeeper opens the gate for Him, and the sheep hear His voice and come to Him. He calls His sheep by name and leads them out. After He gathered his flock, He walks ahead of them, and they follow Him because they recognize His voice. They won't follow a stranger; they will run from a stranger because they don't recognize his voice. See John 10:3-5.

"We will know God's voice. When we become like Jesus, we will love as He does. "My prayer for all of them is that they will be one, just as You and I are one. Father, just as You are in Me, and I am in you they will be in Us, and the world will believe you sent Me." (John 17:21).

Above all else, guard your heart, for it affects everything you do (Proverbs 4:23). Learn to guard your heart. Do not accept anything that is said which does not line up with the Bible. Know who you are in Christ.

When someone says something about you and you know it is not God's Word about you, stop the words coming at you. Perhaps like me, you have heard someone tell you how dumb you were. I was often told as a child "You'll never amount to anything." But now I am a child of God.

I know that His love is more than my mind can comprehend, but I also know that He is so in love with me that those ugly words from childhood do not have any power over my thought life anymore.

Before I left Texas, I went to the courthouse to get some information. I asked the lady working there if I could read the court records about me.

Because of favor with her, she let me read those papers. You see, the words "poor white trash" were something that always stuck in my mind growing up at the children's home and later in life. Sure enough, those very words were written in the files about me.

Then, to hear a doctor say of my future that I would never have children after what my father did to me.

Wrong. I have two beautiful, healthy sons.

To hear I would lose my mind.

Wrong! I've got the mind of Christ!

To hear poor white trash.

Wrong!

To hear that I would never amount to anything.

Wrong!

My Father God is the King of Kings. I belong to Him.

Reject negative words. We never want to come in agreement with someone saying something about us that is not from God's Word.

When we hear something that does not line up with what God says, we can quickly say in our hearts we do not receive that. This is another reason why it is so important to know God's Word.

God wants to be central in our minds. His piece displaces negative words; He wants His Spirit to have control over our hearts and minds at all times. May our thoughts and spoken words be flavored with God's Word.

"Those who love Me inherit wealth, for I fill their treasures." (Proverbs 8:21).

Like me, you can have something that money can't buy. You can have so much peace and joy in life knowing who you are in Him. The love of Jesus is in your heart. He watches over you. He never leaves you nor forsakes you.

"Your enemies will stay far away; you will live in peace. Terror will not come near." (Isaiah 54:14).

God says that your enemies will always be defeated because He is on your side. What you can say is "Thank you, God, for my wonderful life that is covered with the blood and blessings of Christ.

INSPIRATIONAL THOUGHTS

God is a God of the heart. He sees our heart.

Reason is never required. Faith opens the door.

What's in your heart is what comes out.

Obey the Bible and peace will come.

God gave us his Word to make us overcomers in everything.

When you praise God, He will show up.

We are complete now. We are righteous now.

God's word is so full of blessings that always there is a word when we need to hear from Him.

Giving is one of life's greatest blessings. Being a blessing to someone is refreshing.

Following feelings is dangerous. Pressure leads to compromise.

All sin begins with a lie.

THE CELLAR

We stay strong when we stay little in our hearts.

If Jesus had to stop and pray, how much more have we to stop and pray?

Love needs to be released. Everything works by love.

Along with strengths, we also have weaknesses. Let Jesus Christ be strong in your weaknesses; let Him be your strength on your weak days.

Break the power of negative words. Instead, bless people.

We cannot live by feelings nor believe them. Live by the Word of God.

God guides us along the right path bringing honor to his name.

Live out of your spirit.

Give yourself to one thing: seeking the Kingdom of God.

Let God's glory be prominent in your life.

Turn all your problems over to God. Cast all your cares on Jesus.

God loves to hear the sounds of our voices.

Open your heart and let God fix it.

Let us try to remember how we have needed love and forgiveness.

Jesus Christ is God's love gift to the world. And believers are the Father's love gift to Jesus Christ.

God never makes a mistake.

The quieter you become, the more you hear from God. God speaks to our spirit.

Read the Word of God, think of a scripture for the day, and learn to pray around it.

God gave gifts; one is not better than the other.

Praising God means you are thanking Him for what he will do.

Get the Word of God in you to have a life of blessings.

The most damning thing a Christian can do is talk negatively about others.

God's love is the beginning of how to give love and receive. God is love.

Pray about everything.

Whatever God asks you to do, do it.

Let heaven fill your thoughts.

ABOUT THE AUTHOR

Dana Cryer is an accomplished author, speaker, and dedicated Christian. Her life is a living testimony of God's incredible power to deliver. After having suffered several years of mental, physical, and sexual abuse, Dana was on the verge of suicide when God miraculously delivered her, gloriously saved her, and called her to minister to those who are oppressed, abused, and emotionally wounded.

She has a heart for hurting people and has dedicated her life to sharing hope, encouragement, and God's unconditional love to people everywhere. Dana has been married for more than 54 years and has two grown sons.

If this book has ministered to you or helped you in any way, please let Amazon know with a comment and a rating.

PRAYER
HOW TO BECOME A CHRISTIAN

God made the way to Himself simple. If you confess with your mouth that Jesus is Lord and believe in your heart that God raised Him from the dead, you will be saved.

"For it is by believing in your heart that you are made right with God, and it is by confessing with your mouth that you are saved, for everyone who calls on the name of the Lord shall be saved." (Romans 10:9-10, 13 NLT).

"Lord Jesus, I believe you are the Son of God. I believe you came to earth and died on the cross to reconcile humanity to God.

You are Lord, and I believe God raised you from the dead.

I am a sinner, and I am asking you to forgive me of my sins. I will probably fall and sin a few times in this life. But I know you died for my sins and I will always look to you to do better each day.

Thank you, Lord, for coming into my heart.

Amen

Jesus loves you, and so do I, Dana

Find yourself an Amplified Bible and begin reading in the New Testament, Psalms and Proverbs. And find a good Bible-believing church.

THE CELLAR